GOD'S OWN HEART

Poetic Expressions and Affirmations of Edification, Adoration and Exultation

By George L. Hayes

Dorrance Publishing Co
585 Alpha Drive
Suite 103
Pittsburgh, PA 15238
Visit our website at *www.dorrancebookstore.com*

ISBN: 979-8-88812-104-7
EISBN: 979-8-88812-604-2

TABLE OF CONTENTS

ACKNOWLEDGMENTS

As scripted as this may seem, I cannot acknowledge anyone or anything, before giving glory to God! I was given this inspired work for His people, for His glory. All I have, all I am, and all I know, is due to my God! Thanks be to my God and Father! Thanks be to my Lord and Savior, Jesus Christ! I have to acknowledge my parents, giving honor where honor is due. Both were instrumental in my upbringing. My father has been there for me in every way, at every turn, my best man! I am eternally grateful to him. My mother, too, has always been there for me, my main caregiver as a child. May she rest in peace. To my daughter Nyla, my one good thing in this world. She keeps me going. So many people have played integral roles in helping me to become the man that I am today—friends, family, and loved ones. You know who you are. Thank you, and God bless you all!

INTRODUCTION

Congratulations to you, dear reader, on this achievement called life. You are still operating in the land of the living, despite all that this world has thrown at you. Not only are you here, but you are in a prestigious position of pursuing Almighty God. In this collection of poetry, we will explore, expound on, and also edify the Word of God, while gaining understanding of His Heart, His Love for us, and Will for our lives. This collection serves as a great Bible study tool, as each poem is inspired by scripture and contains scriptural references for the reader's application. There are many things in life worthy of pursuing. The older we get, the more clearly we can see what is, or ever was, truly worth our time and attention. Oftentimes, we find that most pursuits were in vain and in fact, a distraction from what we truly should have been going after all along. I pray that you find the things that are truly worth pursuing and attain them. Join with me on this journey, as we chase after "God's Own Heart."

HABITATION

Lost stars, shining their way through the dark. The darkest black covers those who chose darkness. Chains of bondage keep them bound to the ground, awaiting judgment day. Never should have left their habitation!

Paradise visualized, heaven on earth! A habitation made for God and man. A garden full of life and love! Man and woman in innocence, pureness. Such a shame they came to know evil! Now, lost in the light of their own eyes. If the light in their eyes is darkness, why do they still call it light? The lie—bad thought to be good. Good chose to leave because of bad. All is lost! Lost stars, shining their way through the dark. The darkest black covers those who chose darkness. Chains of bondage keep them bound to the ground, awaiting judgment day. Never should have left their habitation!

A name known to all, above all, left His habitation. Put on the chains of darkness. Became the light of the world. Even in this new habitation, the darkness could not comprehend Him. Bled and showed the way to lead others to The Truth. Though some would mock this, through all the darkness, the only true reason for celebration. Thank God He left His habitation!

—Scripture references—
Jude 1:6 and 13; Revelation 1:20, 12:7–12; Genesis 2 and 3 (entire chapter); Matthew 6:23; Isaiah 9:2, 42:16; John 1:4 and 5, 9:5; 1 John 2:11; 1 Peter 2:9; 2 Peter 2:4; Galatians 1:4

BEDSIDE

Sitting bedside with my dear heart. My baby cried and I came running. Just a bad dream, my baby must have had. A baby born; such a beautiful miracle, a love adorn. Life given, addition to the family. If that baby knew the pain of this world, the scorn born into.... Just reminiscing about the beginning of life, but my baby is elderly and the bedside I sit at is a sick bed. My baby cries out again, but this time he's not dreaming. Shrieks of pain, moans and groans! Has already lived longer than they said he would. My baby's suffering so badly! Sometimes I wish his suffering would just end, but then I may never see him again. Been with my baby most of my life. When he goes, I'll probably be following right behind. Had a stroke myself and not in the best of health, but I live to take care of my baby. As if he was a newborn baby, helpless, he needs me. Sleep comes so seldom. Must be ready to always be by my baby's bedside. Lord, my love endures so much pain, seeing my baby fading away from me. Doctors poking and prodding, injecting and cutting into my baby! I don't know if they're making him better or worse. What am I going to do when he leaves me? The Lord gives, The Lord takes away, but what will remain in the end? Lord, please place peace upon my heart. Comfort to know I will be with him again. This is my prayer that I pray, as my baby lays in his sick bed, fading away and I sit by his bedside.

—Scripture References—
Ecclesiastes 3:1–8

SACRIFICE

Spending the summer on my grandpa's farm. Not sure how it will be. Out there so far makes me feel alarm. Grandpa doesn't even think kindly of technology. Maybe if I don't like it, Mama will let me come back early. Here on the farm, got to admit it's awful pretty. I always lived in the South but was raised in the city. Here, you can actually feel the fresh air, so many trees, birds flying everywhere. So peaceful, so beautiful. I think I can get used to this. Kick back on the lake, do a little fishing and swimming.

At least that's what I thought before Grandpa said, "Time to get to working. Feed the pigs, check the crops, clean the pens, and give the pigs more slop. Milk the cow, give the horses some hay, collect the eggs, no time to be lazy." Didn't this man hear, there is no more slavery! The work on this farm is crazy! Always something to do and not four hours after my head hits the bed, I hear, "cock-a-doodle-dooooo!" Then Grandpa says, "Time to get to working. Count the chicks, collect some firewood and sticks...." Going through the barn, I hear wrestling in the sheep's stable. I saw the most amazing thing; a baby being born! Mama licking that baby clean. The baby stumbling and finally making it to unsteady feet. The most amazing thing I've ever seen! Every day from then on, I'm up at the crack of dawn and before Grandpa can say anything, I say, "I know, time to get to working." I race out the door doing my chores extra fast to have extra time to spend in the barn with that newborn baby lamb.

Weeks pass and our bond grows. It seems like she knows when I'm coming and starts calling and kicking at the stall door before I even get there. We would run through the meadows and jump and play. She wasn't really a pet, more like a friend right on time, when it was getting so lonely on the farm. One day, as I entered the barn, I didn't hear my friend calling or kicking. She was gone. By the time I finished the chores and returned to the house, Grandpa said to wash up for dinner. "Lamb tenderloin prepared," and dared to smile when he declared.

"Nooooooo!" I cried. "You killed my only friend! She was just a baby! How could you do such a thing?"

I never shared with Grandpa the time I had been spending with my friend. So he was surprised by my outburst. He said he didn't know. He said, "It is always hard to kill an animal, but better to do it myself than have someone else do it to spare me from the scene. You may believe your hands are clean, but you have become indebted to a man, dependent on another to live. It is better to trust in God than man, working the land, His creation with your own hand, instead of having all your dependence on man-made inventions. Now, I'm sorry you befriended this little lamb, but let's give thanks for its sacrifice and not disgrace it by letting it go to waste."

No, I would not, could not eat my little friend! Just the thought gave me a fright! Needless to say, I went to bed hungry that night. The next day, we attended church. I could not pray; I was still so sad and angry. The preacher began preaching. It was communion and he quoted the scripture that says, "The lamb who was slain for the sins of the world." Could he be talking about my friend? Then he said, "He's a friend that sticks closer than a brother." This is too strange! Had Grandpa been talking to the preacher? He said the disciples called Him "rabbi" which means teacher. Referring to the last supper, he spoke about the sacrifice. Did he mean our super last night? The story of the gospel of Jesus had not yet been familiar to me, but I began to understand that it was God speaking to me! The preacher couldn't know my story, but God did. He orchestrated it! Everything all of a sudden became so clear. God was using all these things to draw me near! The time came for Holy communion. The preacher spoke with the breaking of bread, "Take, eat: this is my body."

Before I ate, I released all resentment toward Grandpa, I ate and felt a peace come over me. The preacher spoke, "This is my blood of the New Testament, that is shed for many." I drank and that grape juice tasted so sweet and gave me goose bumps from my head to my feet! That day, my life was forever changed. There are still times I don't understand things like pain and death. But one thing that I believe, that day God spoke to me. He said, "I am your friend and love you enough to give up My own life. This is My sacrifice!"

—Scripture References—
Revelation 13:8, John 1:49, 3:16 and 6:51–56, 1 John 4:9, Matthew 26:28, 1 Corinthians 11:25, Hebrews 12:24, Romans 8:21

6

SELF-DEFEAT

Self-defeating lusts of the flesh, we embrace. Tastes so sweet, even for a moment. After that moment's passed, lasting wounds and burns create a hole in your soul!

—Scripture references—
1 Corinthians 6:18; 1 Peter 2:11, 4:3; 1 John 2:16 and 17

STORM

Looming over-head, clusters of cumulonimbus clouds take form. Blotting out the sun, sending signs of possible impending doom. Wind gusts whip with destructive force. The atmosphere transformed, signaling the change in weather systems and seasons. There have been many storms to come and pass away. Loud thunder, bright lightning, fierce winds! Whenever they pass, everything seems a little better than before. Trees and plants receive sustenance and life from the rain. Pain produces lessons learned through the storm. Clouds that form always have a silver lining. Passing now, rainbow, sun shining. Promise that this won't be lasting. The brilliance, even brighter colors than before or is it just that I can appreciate it more?

—Scripture References—
Genesis 9:12–16, Isaiah 25:4, 2 Corinthians 4:7–12 and 16–18

RELIGION (HONOR AND CARE)

Loneliness like this makes your insides feel hollow! Emptiness grips you like there's no tomorrow! Memories of better days add a glimmer to your sullen gaze. The older you grow, the more society pushes you into the shadows, not wanting to be reminded of their own mortality. Only finding beauty in the flower of youth. Still, beautiful to see ripe, old age, aging gracefully. So many obstacles overcome, so many accomplishments! Learn from their growing pains and life lessons. Care for them every day. Honor their presence. Most importantly, make sure they know where they'll be spending all eternity! Give back the best blessings after all they've given. Remind them, with love, life's still worth living.

—Scripture Reference—
James 1:27

RELIGION PART 2 (ORPHAN)

No one to care for me, no love around. Feeling lost without ever being found. "Why, nobody's looking for me?" Shuffled place to place without a place to call my own. Orphaned and alone! Heart growing cold to prevent the pain that always remains! "I don't care that nobody loves me!" But I do. Create pictures in my head of a family I never knew. Something is breaking inside me. About to turn me into somebody I don't want to be! "If God is real, where is He? If He really loves me, why don't I have a family?" A Christian love blossoms and then comes marriage. But time passes and still no baby carriage. Doctors determine this young couple, unable to bear the blessing of bringing a baby into the world. They would not even consider any artificial means of conceiving; they believe if done unnaturally, it would go against God. So, all seems lost! The one thing both dreamed and hoped for. "God, how could you do this to us? Everything is a total bust! Now, all we do is argue and fuss!" Two needs can be met, and God can be glorified by joining these separate circumstances. All past regret, resentment, and disappointment laid aside. Visit the orphan in his time of need. Pray, God grants you a match made in heaven, predestined. This was always your destiny. Finally, a family!

—Scripture Reference—
James 1:27

RELIGION PART 3 (SPOTLESS)

Stains, spots, dirty, and ashamed! Bloodstained, drops of sinful transgression! The world paints an evil picture, your life connects the dots. An abstract mess on your shirt. Must confess, that's a hideous dress! Wanting to enter the great party celebration, but no way you are getting in, looking that way! To reach the party, you went in the wrong direction anyway, turning away in shame! Just then, you're reminded of the miraculous cleaner that washes your garment, removing every stain, making it bright white again! You know Him by name. You call Him, and He comes to you to do the impossible. "Before you go," He does address, "remember the ways that led your dress to look such a mess. Go now, and sin no more!"

—Scripture Reference—
James 1:27

DIZZY DOGS

The pursuit of happiness, first and foremost, in this life. As a dog chasing his tail. Leaving you dizzy, disappointed, disillusioned, and dismayed.

—Scripture References—
Matthew 16:26, Luke 12:16–21

CURSES

Curses, curses, curses! Cursed to travail through much pain! The ground cursed, cursed to be vain! Cursed in separation from the Almighty! Cursed in death, in iniquity! Generational curses, binding, intertwining, combining! Curses compounding! I hate this world! Finding solace, peace, and rest in He who became the curse for me, that I might be free, that I might be blessed!

—Scripture References—
Genesis 3:14–19; Deuteronomy 21:23; Psalm 51:5; Isaiah 14:21, 53:5; Galatians 3:13

CHRIST LIFE

To live is Christ! Life given back to The Giver. Practicality of work, transformed spiritually, magnified exponentially! To die is gain! Martyrs spark a mighty movement, igniting the people when the righteous are slain! The first death, not to be feared. The righteousness of God in Christ Jesus, will rise, resurrected, transformed, reconnected, forever to dwell with the Lord! If you treasure and cherish this life, you're at risk of tasting the second death! Wailing, sobbing, gnashing of teeth! Tormenting through all eternity! With free will, decide, bondservant of Jesus the rest of this life. All other things be profane. To live is Christ! To die is gain!

—Scripture References—
Philippians 1:21, 3:8, 4:13, Galatians 2:20, Romans 6:4–11, 2 Corinthians 5:17, 1 Thessalonians 4:13–17, John 11:25, Matthew 25:30, Revelation 2:11, 6:9–11, 17:6, 20:6, 21:8,

CORE VALUE

Better to put your trust in God than man. Even though you may not believe it so, this poem's intention is for the already saved Christian. The very center of the Bible, Psalm 118:8 states this as a most important fact. If thought that this, being the centerpiece of the Bible, is chance or happenstance, further evidence is given with simple addition. There are exactly 594 chapters before Psalm 118, 594 chapters after. Add those chapters together, you get the total 1188, pointing back to Psalm 118:8. That proves this verse is of extreme significance, point-blank! Total dependence on society is the ultimate trap! God's creation provides all the provisions for man. As provisions are given, find your own promised land. Question—what if, one day, you couldn't feed yourself, your family, not be able to buy or sell in society without compromising your Christianity? Better to put your trust in God than man. The road of the world will lead all mankind to damnation! They make everything so convenient, but in the end, enslavement. Money, sex, drugs, and entertainment has always been, now, technology is the idol of today. Through industrialization, a secular society has become our only means of survival! The Bible has so many references to agriculture and farming for a reason, more than just being a part of the Hebrew culture. Our own laziness has backed us into a corner. You may think your trust is not in man, but if you do, think again! If "do to others as you would have them do to you" is the golden rule, then, "better to put your trust in God than man" ought to be our core value! This is not symbolic but is meant for practical application. If there was anything to get, get this! If the point wasn't made, in case you didn't understand, better to put your trust in God than man!

—Scripture References—
Psalm 118:8, Hebrews 11:9, Ecclesiastes 7:29, Exodus 3:17, Revelation 13:16 and 17

CORE VALUE (part 2)

A religion made by man cannot stand! But in the land of iniquity, we see the unholy trinity of me, myself and I. If it's not about me, it does not apply. The light in your eyes, truly darkness. Hate, not the opposite of love, it's selfishness. Love always gives, the love of money always takes. Man, self-exalting, building inventions bringing us closer to the Heavens, but farther from God! Where or when will it end! Men, mindless sheep following society wherever they lead. It's better to trust in God than man. Patient endurance needed to finish this race. Lack of knowledge leaves you vulnerable. Mindless sheep following any Shepard. Blind leading the blind, or sinister plans plunging you into outer darkness. In the end you won't be let in. Outside you will be left to face a place with much wailing and gnashing of teeth! Now, you can save yourselves from incomprehensible grief! Though necessary to obey the laws of the land, at every turn, make sure your trust is in God, not man!

—Scripture References—
James 3:13–16, Philippians 1:7 and 2:3, Galatians 5:19–21, 2 Timothy 3:1–5, Psalm 118:8

RESTORE THE STOREHOUSE

Where is the storehouse of the Lord? The storehouse the bible speaks of. Why is there no food in God's house? The tenth, the tithe brought in from men and women. Where are the farmlands, rich in grain, fruits and vegetables? Vast lands with all types of animals, good for meat, good to eat. We've deserted the land, God's creation. Money cannot be the only form of currency, in God's storehouse, though the love of money has caused this to be. My Father's house has turned into a den of thieves! Everything is always about money. Restore the storehouse of the Lord! Return to God's creation, no longer solely focused on man-made inventions. Every generation looks sadly at the next generation to come. Morals and values, so much degeneration! Way of life, lifestyles priorities shifted. So far removed from the simple life, it may seem absurd to return. If you only knew the trap set for you. Continuing down this path the world has laid out for you, where they prefer the synthetic and virtual over the real! Wide and broad, for many to travel, but the end, destruction!

—Scripture References—
Malachi 3(entire chapter), Matthew 7:13, Revelation 13:16 and 17, 14:9–12, Ecclesiastes 7:29,1 Timothy 6:10, 2 Timothy 3:1–5, Jeremiah 7:11, Luke 19:46, Psalm 118:8

A NAME

What's in a name? Some, given by parents. Some, by God. Some, assigning assignments, identifying identity and purpose. Adam, meaning "red earth." The first man in creation, formed from the dust. Timothy, "one who fears God." Not hard to see God's wisdom placed in his identity. Daniel meaning, "God is my judge." Even standing subject to the king of the land, he would not bow down, knowing God had all power In His hand! Abraham, "father of many nations." A name given directly from God. He also revealed to me, the name that reveals my destiny. Last male to legitimately carry my last name. Everyone previously carrying my first name, in my family, carried the mantle for our legacy. First name, George, "farmer," where I find my purpose. Visions given of much land promised. That's right, I said a promised land, to provide for God's people, when we can no longer conform to society. When society forces conformity on our forehead or hand. For surely, it is better to trust in God than man! Middle name, Leonard, "brave as a lion." Last name, Hayes, "lives by the forest." That's exactly where you'll find me. So exciting to see God showing my identity wrapped up in my name! I would be remiss if I neglected to mention the Name above all names! Jesus, "God the Savior!" Christ, "The Messiah, The Anointed One!" Appointed to die for the sins of the world! Find meaning in your life. Find the meaning of your name. Leaning on the master, congregating corporately or in seclusion, one name we all share. Baptized by water, Spirit and fire, we all stand, CHRISTIAN!

—Scripture References—
Philippians 2:9, Genesis 17:5–7, Acts 1:5 and 3:16, Exodus 20:7

DEEP DOWN INSIDE

Deep in my heart, I cry! In my spirit, there's a pain that flows so deep! These tears, this pain, not for me, but all the lost of the world. My soul sighs, deep down inside, in the inward parts, where You taught me wisdom! I found the light that gave me sight to find the right road. Still, scarcely saved myself. Still can't help but think about those, so many still lost in the dark forest, full of ravenous wolves, insidious snakes, and destructive dragons! Deep down inside, I find the same light in me, that gave me sight, that guided me to the right road. How do I dial up this light, get it to shine very bright? Where would be the best place to stand, to shine down on all mankind? If I go there, the Destroyer may see me too, putting myself in harm's way. Deep down inside, I find a selfless love, none greater, willing to lay down my life, for my brother. I sacrifice this vessel, living and unto death. In position, light shining bright! I pray you find the same light that I found, deep down inside.

—Scripture References—
Matthew 5:14, Romans 12:1, John 3:19, 8:12, 12:46, 15:13, 2 Corinthians 4:6–12, Acts 13:47, Revelation 12(entire chapter), 1 Peter 4:18, Psalm 51:6

THE KEY

Understanding knowledge and wisdom combined. Puts me ahead in the race. Divining the path, discerning the pace. Avoiding landmines. Standing firm by grace. God would that all could be saved. Not wanting any to perish. Still, people are perishing for lack of knowledge. Lacking the Word of Life. The Word of salvation that should be embedded in your soul. Faith comes by hearing the Word, wisdom too. Knowledge and understanding, yes, they all do. People perishing, worse than any earthly war. To come into the house, all you need to do is open the door. To gain heavenly wisdom, open up the book. Could gain access to Your Highness so easily and be saved! Joining God's family! Though courage and bravery are needed for this journey, knowledge is key!

—Scripture References—
Hosea 4:6 and 7; Proverbs 4 (entire chapter), 18:15; 2 Peter 1:2–5; Philippians 1:9; Luke 11:52; Colossians 2:2–5, 3:10; 1 Corinthians 1:21, 2:6; Ecclesiastes 7:12

STILL HERE

Strong winds still blow over me. My storm's not over, even though they told me it would be. Raining pain, down on me! Winds and rain, thunder and lightning, all crashing down on me! Out in the elements, all forms show wear and tear, from the storm. Mud slides, erosion. Even sharp rocks smoothed, over time. So why am I still here? Not by power or might. Worn, weather torn, every night, but renewed in brand new mercies, every day! Storms come and go, and I know they will come again. Don't need anybody to prophesy on me, that my storm is over. I will stay on guard, always guarding my heart, not knowing where or when the next storm will blow in. I cannot adopt worldly theologies, wanting this life to be easy, never experiencing pain and fear. In a world ruled by the enemy, in a state of war, that's just not reality. All I know is, kept by grace and mercy, I'm still here!

—Scripture References—
Proverbs 4:23, 7:1, Deuteronomy 4:9, Hosea 12:6, Hebrews 4:16, Ephesians 2:7, Psalm 57:1, Isaiah 32:1 and 2

DESPERATION

Desperation I'm facing, continually chasing after You. Pursuing something true that will make me brand new. Running from my past in the shadows, all the shallow that won't last. Temporal temptations, promising gratification. Only leaving you emptier than before but still searching for more and more. Entangled, in bondage, enslaved again. Can't win for losing! How did I get here? Was running so well. What did hinder you, put you under a spell? Born into sin, shaped in iniquity. A righteous man falls seven times but rises to life more abundantly. So, in the desperation which I'm facing, I will continue chasing after You. Pursuing Someone true, the Truth which makes me brand new.

—Scripture References—
Galatians 5:7, Psalm 42:1, 2 Peter 2:20, 1 Corinthians 10:13, James 1:13, Luke 8:13, Philippians 3:13, Proverbs 24:16

THANKFUL

Thankfulness flows out of the river of my soul. Charged up, gracefully, by Your Spirit, thankfully. Enamored by You and, yes, thankful too. So many blessings given. Too many blessings to count. With each passing day, You become more amazing to me! So thankful for a loving family. So thankful for all other loved ones too. Thankful for food, clothing and shelter, life, health, and strength. The Blood of the Lamb, flowing all the way through. Thank You for blessings I don't even know. All You do behind the scenes. Thank You for work and the ability, activity of my extremities. Good works, ministry, storing up my treasures eternally. So thankful that Your hand is upon me, that You gave me an extra set of eyes to see spiritually. Thank You for edification in the body, for traveling mercies, justification, sanctification through my mind. Living in a free nation. Salvation, Grace, forgiveness...What did I miss? So much to be thankful for. Thank You for this food that's getting cold cause I can't stop thanking You, just so thankful!

—Scripture References—
1 Timothy 2:1-6, 4:4; Philippians 4:4-7; Psalm 69:30, 95:25, 100:4; 2 Corinthians 4:15; Jeremiah 30:19; Ephesians 5:4

SELF-JUSTIFIED

Righteous in your own sight, self-justified. Might just be your own light, is that of foolish pride. None have done enough good works to clean their stains of sin. Everyone guilty of some transgression. So, you stand in the flesh, apart from Christ, the one who died, self-justified. The problem is, you do not have the judgment seat, or authority. You've returned to the law, forsaking His Spirit, which is your guarantee. You cannot accomplish anything that will endure, apart from the Lord. The self-justified, still found condemned, because self has no heaven or hell to place you in!

—Scripture References—
Ecclesiastes 7:16, Luke 18:9–14, 2 Corinthians 1:22, Romans 3(entire chapter), Galatians 3(entire chapter), Philippians 3(entire chapter)

CARPE DIEM

Carpe Diem—seize the day! Proactively take charge and do not play! When the studying is done, it's time to put it into action. Pull out your sword and start slashing! That devil right there, wanted to put a wedge between you and your family. Divide and conquer was His plan, but, still, you stand in unity. Offensively, deciding to slash to pieces all the snares of the enemy. Not waiting for him to come into the home, meet him out on the front line and defeat with authority! Back him down, lay him down! Put him under your feet, accordingly! If, by now, you're not sure if that devil is dead, take out that sword and whack him on his head! The Word of God shows you just what to do. Take up your double-edged sword and get in the battle too. Take back everything the devil's stolen from you. How many days do you think you have on this earth? For what it's worth, seventy summers, eighty winters, does not a lot yield. Better make them count down on the battlefield. Put on the full armor before you step into battle. Speak bold, in Jesus' name and watch their cages rattle. Speak blessings over our habitation, future generations, and leaders of the nations. Pray that your love shows true to God and people too. Because without love, Our Father has nothing to do with you. We are known by our love. Knowing money, sex, drugs, and all the other lusts keep us out of the battle, actually forcing us to fight for the losing side. Did I mention pride? We need His Spirit as our guide, working with the Sword of His word. Awareness is key, keeping Him in the front of your mind. Don't let the world lull you to sleep and waste your time. Let the Lord use you from the soles of your feet to the crown of your head. The way He uses me, I slay one thousand demons before I even leave the bed!

—Scripture References—
Revelation 1:16, Hebrews 4:12, Romans 16:20, Ephesians 6:13, 1 John 4:16

NO REGRETS

Been walking, working, talking Christ, this whole new life, and still have no regrets! Been studying, meditating, focused on Christ, a long time now, but still find new, that makes me, "wow!" Been fighting, running, wrestling, gunning. Picking my battles, or the Lord picks them for me. Fighting the good fight, does often leave me weary. Battle scarred, I thank God, He gives me rest, my strength renewed. Been doing this here for a long time now. When I forget and lose my way, I'm reminded, the solid rock, the only place to stay. No matter how hard things get, how hurt I get, I still have no regrets. Even when lack strikes a chord. Whatever I don't have, I don't need. I'm Just so grateful I have the Lord!

—Scripture References—
Isaiah 40:31, Hebrews 12:28, Colossians 3:15, 1 Thessalonians 5:18, 2 Thessalonians 2:13, 1 Timothy 1:12, 6:12, Ephesians 6:12

REDEEM

Wild and fierce, feeding the beast in me! Feeding frenzy! Drunken brawls, pointless contests. Who's the best at being their worst? The beast in me, carnal bestiality. Marking my territory. Mounting every piece of tail I see, that appeals. The dog in me, sexual immorality. Coarse jesting, professing much profanity. The fool in me, my frivolous illegality. Coveting everything I see, wanting much more than I need. The pig in me, my greedy activities. No one so undone has any place in the Kingdom of Heaven! I have had them all, or they all had me, until the Lord God Almighty, did set me free! So now, child of light, no longer dwell in darkness. Redeem the times, for the days are evil. Idol hands, enticing traps, kidnaps you back into the very things you died to! Demons resurrected seven-fold! Familiarity breeds backsliding. Old habits, so hard to break. Addictions take hold, again! Struggling with the same sins you were found with in the beginning! Returning to mere milk. You should be eating meat, making the most of each moment, stirring up treasures, tipping the scales and measures, for God's Glory! Proving yourself worthy. Evil are the times, don't let that be your story. Tomorrows promised to no one. Redeem the days, while it's still called today! When all is said and done, I just want to make it into Heaven! Accomplish everything He ordained for me. Amen, times ten!

—Scripture References—
Ephesians 5(entire chapter), James 4:13–17, 1 Corinthians 3:1–3, Matthew 6:19 and 20, 2 Timothy 1:6, Isaiah 56:11, Romans 6:2, 13:13, Galatians 5:21, 1 Peter 4:3,

SEASON

This is the season of bountiful blessings; this is the season of great gain! Though always blessed, this time is special, a time to enjoy exponential increase! Pour now, shower celebrations of blessings! Fulfilling everything foretold, with good works predestined. This is the season of anointing! God appointing importantly, poignantly, to bring forth His Glory. This is our season, our people perpetually prospering! We will reap the rewards of love, enduring through much pain and suffering. Never heard this in a song, but love suffers long! Pregnant with purpose, driving forth conceived substance. Many labors, labor pains. Producing God's Glory with every strain. Contractions come, constricting, conflicting, pain consuming, in the womb, coming down the birth canal. With production of life, comes much sacrifice. Made it through trimester after trimester, one upon another, to the ultimate climax! Though I find myself on my back, still fighting, still pushing! Life gives life with a struggle so debilitating, it almost takes your life. Breath in lungs, almost perforating! Breathe, breathe, push! Finally, the arrival prophesied! Entering a foreign land, will this conceived substance be received! This foreign land found to be claimed by the enemy. The enemy identifies and pursues, as soon as he arrives on the scene. Floods of people sent in for the purpose of theft, death and destruction. Still, Life will accomplish what Love sacrificed for. Truth will endure! Celebrating birth of life, but the celebration be for all seasons, all time, knowing the end, from the beginning! This is the season ordained by God! Though trials be hard, more than worth it for the birth of sons and daughters of God. The birth of a business, to the Glory of God. The birth of an anointed book, speaking God's truths. So many things being birthed, bringing forth truth, love and life. You may even find yourself pregnant with purpose right now. Join with the greatest birth of all, that of The Christ!

—Scripture References—
Revelation 12(whole chapter), Luke 2:1–21, 1 Corinthians 13:4, Ephesians 2:10, Hebrews 10:24, Matthew 5:16, 24:4–8, Galatians 4:19, Genesis 3:16

BLINDED

Blind fear, afraid of what you cannot see! Darkness conceals footsteps that follow me. Fearing the unknown. Heart's racing! Picking up the pace, I begin running. Footsteps start chasing! "If I could just see what's behind me, I'd know what to do. Is this thing trying to prevent me from reaching my destination?" More than one pursuer, I perceive shadows lurking everywhere! Sets of eyes in the bushes, fixed on me. Shivers take control of my body! Ominous sounds, shrieks, moans, howls and growls. Shadows approaching, getting closer now. Something's on the prowl, hunting me down! I drop down low. "Since I can't see, maybe they won't see me either." Closer and closer the sounds, the footsteps, the shadows. Like scared prey, rattled from their hiding place, I dash! Sprinting past all that means harm to me. Coming into the light of the moon. Clear, calm, cool. Collecting myself. Seems all of them things went away. Clouds ambush the moon, blotting out the light! Darkness returns, blindness reforms, with shadows all around! "Did they ever leave?" Sounds begin to groan and moan, howl and growl again. Footsteps this time, seem like they're galloping! Better start running! Stumbling over what I cannot see. I feel elevated as I run. I have reached the top of a hill. Sounds seem to be all around. Even hearing screams now! Could that be another victim they capture before me? Claws digging in the ground climbing up the mound, the hill. I'm totally surrounded, nowhere to go! Darkness concealed what Truth would reveal. The light is in you! On the hill, the perfect place to shine. Divine treasures, in you, begin to stir. Compressing, convoluting, converging! Just when the shadows lurking reach the top of the hill, this vessel, full of Holy Ghost power, ignites! Shining so bright, no foe could withstand. Obliterating all dark forces in every direction! Shining so bright, everyone that could see, would have to give God Glory!

—Scripture References—
James 4:7, Matthew 5:14–16, Ephesians 6:12, 2 Timothy 1:6

NEVER ENOUGH

Just a little more, please! The disease of discontentment. Never enough received, never enough spent. Money, never enough. The More your supply, the more demand. The homeless, still homeless, but you're on your way up, upgrade after upgrade. Even at the pinnacle, it's never enough. Two family home with 56 rooms. Still looking to expand. Greed comes in many forms, but money serves them all, burning fast in your hand. Tables turn, now you're in money's grasp. Never thought it would happen to you. You've fallen in love, speak so highly of. Laying in the bed with it, even kissing it. Money, must always have it, so you'll never miss it.

Never enough sex, never enough sex partners. The flesh, never satisfied, the More conquests, the more pride. Tried every freaky thing to try to bring more satisfaction and excitement. Just the regular sex has become boring. Vanity, puffed up with your chest puffed out. Stud with the ladies. Not satisfied until you get an STD. Body diseased, deformities created by the disease of discontentment. Insatiable desires drive you to dangerous decisions, going out on a limb with a branch already broken. The fall, just a matter of time. Still surprised, in your mind. Never thought it would happen to you. After falling victim to disease and decay, your appetite still urges, you still want to play. The vicious cycles continue. Temptation promises pleasure without disclosing consequence.

Never enough drugs, never enough alcohol. Just looking to relax, relieve the stress. Need a release, get away, that's all. Every once in a while, no more no less. Every day, soon, your drugs will call. More and more often, 'til you're craving all the time. Whatever you had, now has you! To think, all this began with mere curiosity. Insatiably consumed in addiction, chasing fantasy transformed to terror! Surprised how you got here. Never thought it would happen to you. A black hole is sucking the life out of your soul and your body. A shell of your former self. Overtaken by your desire for drugs, necessities like food and hygiene, neglected. Killing you, but still can't get enough. A slave, you have become, driving you to destruction.

Never get enough of Your Spirit! Never get enough of Your Love! Distractions always grab me away, but with You is where I want to stay. Never enough learning about You! The more I learn, the more I want to know! Your symmetry, in nature, is simply incredible! The hierarchy of animals, and plants! The harmony of life, intense! Never learn enough, and I doubt I ever will. Still, in the land of iniquity it's a "dog eat dog" world. Reminds me why I never get enough of Your Spirit, or enough of Your Love. Because we're not together as a family, in unity. That void has caused me to get caught up in money, sex and drugs. Never thought it would happen to me. But I have hit a brick wall, have had enough of chasing things that make me fall. I'll just take whatever I can get from You, even though I never get enough. Maybe, all eternity will be. We'll just have to wait and see. Until that moment, Lord please deliver me from the disease of discontentment!

—Scripture References—
Proverbs 27:20, Ecclesiastes 5:10, 6:7, 11:10, Isaiah 56:11, 1 Peter 4:3, 2 Peter 2:14, Romans 13:13, Galatians 5:21,

SECRET PLACE

Spiritual exercise keeps your soul ties strongly connected to your Creator, causing profitability in virtually everything. Simple as a song you sing. But first, let's back this up, preparing for the warmup. Oh, how I relish these moments! Going to really enjoy this. Go into your closet, alone, privately. Your secret place, special to you and you know Who. Quietly enjoy quality quiet time as you clear your mind. Breathe deeply, relaxing more with every exhale. Speak freely, listening to the words unveil. Quiet, sweet, soft whispers on bended knees. Hairs on the back of my neck stand up, goose bumps all over my body! Meditations on my mediator and great intercessor, Lord and Savior, Jesus Christ. Speaking boldly, in Jesus' name, to the Creator of all life. Father God, I proclaim, hallowed be Thy Name! Blessed Spirit, like fire shut up in my bones! The energy, so sweet to me. The intensity grows, groans inexplicably unexplainable! Speaking in languages even foreign to me! The weight of this, pushing me down to the ground! I lay prostrate, immense amounts of power flowing through me now! Out of my mouth, as I speak, I feel power leaving me. Out of my hands, I stretch them wide and up, wave them side to side. Heat pulsating through my fingertips! Toes grip the carpet in a tight clench! So much power flowing now, and it feels so fine! Drops of sweat dripping down my face. Clothes even wet, but not a single regret. So intimate, the time spent, in my prayer closet.

—Scripture References—
Psalm 91:1; Matthew 6:6; Luke 11:2; Deuteronomy 9:18; John 7:38; 1 Timothy 4:8; 1 Corinthians 12:10, 12:28; Luke 8:43–48

SPEAK OUT

Speak out! Speak out to each other! Speak out to each other, in psalms and hymns, making melody, with all your heart, to The Lord! The Lord spoke and commanded, speak out to each other, in this manner. It is a matter of fact, that the manner in which we often speak is shameful, not for Godly people. Speak God's Word, words of power and love. Words of edification, praise and admonition. Why do you speak the language of fear and doubt, forsaking the author and finisher of your faith? Speaking foolishly, gossips and busybodies. Small thinking, small talk. God should be represented by your speech and walk. The body of Christ, creating schisms and strife, should solely be speaking life. Rectification within the body begins with this very thing! If turned off by the antiquity of His Word, iniquity has consumed you! Wanting everything to be handed to you. Instead, you should be chasing after the God that chased after you. If meditative thought processes give you access and help expose and reveal all that fill your soul with all good things, though antiquated the Word may be, He'll give you a new song to sing. Filling yourself with His Spirit, His living Word. Then speak out! Speak out to each other! Speak out to each other, in psalms and hymns, making melody with all your heart, to the Lord!

—Scripture References—
Ephesians 5:19, Colossians 3:16, 1 Timothy 5:13

ALIEN

An alien in a foreign land ruled by the enemy. The best story is reality. My story, otherworldly. Simultaneously coexisting in two dimensions, transcendence. Each dimension influencing the other. One made for the Creator. Spiritual, heavenly, eternal. Though beyond my grasp, transcendentally, I attain my heavenly treasure. God and His Word created everything in six days. The seventh day reserved for rest, reflection, and praise. Now my words, ringing true, can produce too—building blocks in eternity, for the up-building of His Kingdom. Simultaneously living in a physical vessel, in a fallen world. Not quite hell but far from heaven. Still standing for righteousness. Standing out like a sore thumb. Praying as His kingdom comes, may His will be done. Heaven descending means world elevation. No longer separate but consolidating. All creation's been waiting, moaning, even groaning in eager expectation. No longer alien, all things rectified. Unity in the body, connected to the head. In humble adoration, restoration realized. No more contemplating. I am a child of the Most High!

—Scripture References—
John 18:36; Ephesians 2:2, 6:12; Romans 8:22 and 23; Proverbs 18:12; Genesis 1 (entire chapter), 2:1–3; Hebrews 11:13; Matthew 6:10

MERCY

I will be glad and rejoice in Your mercy. Hope to, one day, be in Your Glory. Lord, have mercy! Let the lying lips cease, let the righteous increase. Put an end to all Your enemies! Lord, have mercy! I have not hidden my iniquity. For each and every sin, please forgive me! Lord, have mercy! Shout for joy, the upright in heart! He loved us from the start! Lord, have mercy! Blessed is the nation whose God is the Lord, who hopes in His mercy. My soul boasts in the Lord, for His eyes are upon me. Every new day, I find brand new mercies! Thank You, Lord God Almighty! Thank You for Your Mercy!

—Scripture References—
Psalm 31, Lamentations 3:23, 2 Corinthians 3:18, 1 Samuel 20:16

IN SYNC

To worship You, I live. I pour out my soul; I give You control. My heart yearns to be close to You! Inner joy, coming from the source of it all, shining through! Rivers of life flowing now too. All I am is in love with You! Blessings flowing through me to accomplish all that brings glory to the Almighty with edification, sanctification, and intercessions to the body. Power flowing through my hands now as I lift them up to You. In my feet, I feel a dance now as I'm moving to the beat. Rhythm and flow, rhythm and flow. In sync, corporately becoming one body. To worship You, we live. Such beauty, such bliss, getting lost in this. If praising You is what I was made to do, I don't want to do anything else. Locked in a moment in time, I close my eyes and time stops! Elevated with the hosts in heaven. Joining them in humble adoration. Nothing else even matters at all! High off your Spirit, nothing compares! Jubilation, celebration, and what elation! I live to worship You!

—Scripture References—
1 Timothy 2:8; Psalm 63:3, 66:4, 134:2; 2 Samuel 6:14; John 7:38

GLORY CHASER

Glory chaser! Fortune and fame, the name of the game. Self-exalting be the story. No guts, no glory! Learning to bend men's might and will to yours. Conniving deceitful, thriving off other's weakness. Bow down, give me the crown! One step closer to ultimate victory! A man that can stand against the whole world, and win, what glory can be found in him! Whatever division, a bona fide world champion! If you exalt yourself, you will be humbled. In humility, learned glory belongs to God alone! An Angel came near and whispered in my ear," Be of good cheer, Jesus has overcome the world!" Not forcing men to bend their might and will to His. He came down, out of Glory, and gave up the crown. Made the greatest story ever told, not by exalting Himself, but humbling Himself to that of a servant, selflessly! Wow, He did show me the way! No more selfish glory chasing! No more self-exalting. Now I serve, in humility, subduing my flesh, by His Spirit. Much more power, in this, than when I walked alone! Became a part of something so much greater than I. Now that my steps are properly ordered, I will not be denied! As You sit high upon Your throne, You Will be glorified!

—Scripture References—
John 6:41, Mark 10:45, Ephesians 3:13, Psalm 119:12

SACRIFICE OVER COMFORT

Most people choose comfort over sacrifice, striving for the lavish life. Following in the footsteps of Jesus, lays the path of sacrifice over comfort, obedience over sacrifice. Following this path of obedience and sacrifice, it seems the more you give up, the more you gain. I almost feel guilty, as I grab treasures, to be stored up for me in Glory! Gaining treasures, growing in humility. You teach us patience, in taking it one day at a time. Not getting ahead of our daily mercies. Following this path that Jesus laid out for us, gives us the greatest companion for this journey, cause He's walking right along with me! Even when sacrifice leads me through pain, trials teach me to be strong. Endurance needed to make it to the end of our path. Though we weep at moments of weakness, it won't last long. At these weak moments, God's strength is perfected, as we keep our faith in Him, our focus on Him, that laid out the path, from beginning to end. As we approach our darkest night, we are closest to the dawn, gaining sight in new light, reminding us, we chose right!

—Scripture References—
Psalm 23, Isaiah 15:22, Hebrews 13:15, Romans 12:1, 2 Corinthians 12:9, Matthew 10:22

FORTRESS

A shipwreck survivor, floating on a piece of wood. So glad that I was not mentioned amongst the dead. A building demolished with one blow. To know I had business there that day, makes me awfully thankful! Just passed six cars crashed that occurred simultaneously, just a minute ago. Good thing I took that extra minute to go back in the house and turn out the lights. In the midst of warfare, bullets fly everywhere, but none hit me. People drop like flies, left and right, right beside me! Still, I stand. My fortress fortified, with the Lord on my side, no harm shall befall me. Even when self-destructive, with a bad attitude, kicking stones. Throbbing pains remain in my toes to teach me never to do it again. He heard my cry and brought me up out of the pit. Was stuck in sticky clay, but now, I can say He placed me on the solid Rock and for-tified me in His fortress this day!

—Scripture References—
Psalm 91(entire chapter), 116:1; 1 Corinthians 12:4

BENEATH THE SURFACE

Go a little deeper, find the buried treasure. On the surface, goods to be found. Underneath the surface, much more profound! The deeper you go, treasure becomes immeasurable. So far down, most shallow people left at the surface, lost in the glare of blindness. Only chasing what they see, in love with money, but can't see past their bellies! If they could just unearth this, and get into dark tunnels, their light will begin to shine. Tunneling now, beneath the ground. Deep calls to deep. If you delve into the depths of truth, you will find more than meets the eye. If your search goes deep down into this ground, much more than just poems to be found. Immeasurable treasures stored up for you in Glory. Peace, protection, provisions. Become a part of the greatest story ever told! Avoid landmines and landslides, to keep you buried deep down beneath the ground! Learn, deep beneath the surface, who truly stands for what. At the surface devils dance as angels, plots, attacks from all angles! To truly know your enemy, to be able to see him when he's coming, you must unearth this, BENEATH THE SURFACE!

—Scripture References—
Philippians 3:19, 2 Corinthians 4:7, Matthew 6:19–21

THIS TIME

An old bum at the park looks on at a young loving couple. Flirting, kissing, and playing with such affection and love. He begins reminiscing of younger days—dapper, debonair, intelligent, talented. At one point in time, the world was at his feet. A complete stud! Was always good with the women; the women were always good to him. So, he took advantage, squandering his talents, living off the sweat of another's brow. Began taking drugs and would not, could not relent. Relying on looks and charisma to get him what he wanted. Time passed, looks faded, money didn't last. His health degraded, and life passed him by. Nothing to show for it, so much regret! As he was looking at the couple, tears began to drop from his eyes. He wished he could go back and do it all over again. This time, he would choose Love, this time he would win! As he was crying, a sensation, a pain unfamiliar, hit him. He was dying! Just then, a voice hearkened unto him. Tim, today you have finally seen the error in your ways. Your heart, now, is finally prepared for Me. Love's always been knocking at the door of your heart. Let Me in, so true love can start.

—Scripture References—
2 Chronicles 12:14; Psalm 10:17, 51:10

MY SHEPHERD

Little bow peep and me, a dumb sheep. Chasing tail because my flesh tells me to, and reproducing is what dumb animals do. Because I'm a follower, I'll follow another off a cliff. Put on a certain attitude just because that's what the masses do. Poor dumb sheep in a world full of sin, a world full of ravenous wolves. Flocking together for protection but just attracting destruction. When the flock is together, the wolves come running. One young wolf at the top of a hill spots the flock in view. Wants to run down and get a few in the valley. The wise old wolf knows just what to do, knows just how to rally. The prince of subtle deceit, such patient contemplating, so plotting. Instead of running, walk down slowly while they're grazing. Build a fence around the whole flock. By the time they look up, we would have corralled all the sheep, running with little bow peep. Now we've got them in the belly of the beast! Just when things began to look so bleak, Mary had a little Lamb. The prophesied sheep. His fleece was white as snow with a Holy Ghost glow. Slain for the sins of the world, beaten black and blue. Blood red, He shed for you. Rose again and gained the crown and all the power too. Now, The Lord is my Shepherd, and He is so good to me! He sets all the dumb sheep free, who were tangled up in sin, corralled once again. Now free to live life abundantly. Green pastures, still waters, and safety, for thou art with me and will never forsake me. Even preparing me for royalty in the presence of my enemies. Though ravenous wolves still may be following me to see if I fall off the righteous path, goodness and mercy follow me too to see that I never do. Now, a sheep might not be too clever, but because he knows his Master's voice, he gets to dwell in the kingdom of God forever!

—Scripture References—
Psalm 23 (entire chapter), Matthew 10:16, Isaiah 6:8, John 8:47, 1 John 2:2

MY #1 EVERYTHING

God is my #1, my #1 everything! God is, in everything, the best! Every good thing, lay aside the rest. God is, in law, the very best lawyer. When up against Him, there is no contest. God is my #1 friend forever, better than a brother! Nurtures and trains me better than a mother. When talking of a lover, no love greater than to lay His life down for a sinner. God is the best GPS, navigating through the road of life. Traveling mercies to see you through. Grace to help you do the impossible! God is the best defense against attacks I can't see. Giving me authority offensively, to put the enemy under my feet. When I am sick in my body, the balm in Gilead shows up right on time! A doctor with a cure for everything malign. Miracles to bear witness that God is the best. He's the #1 Father, especially to the fatherless. Simply The best of the best! Don't understand people that don't know Him, can't see Him. Singing songs about anything. God is the only song to sing. God is my #1, my #1 everything!

—Scripture References—
1 John 4:10, Psalm 68:5, John 14:26, Ephesians 1:18–23

FOCUS

Seems hopeless, keeping my mind stayed on You, though focus is what You've commanded me to do. When I hear your name, when I think about you, something resonates inside me, rising up from within! Still, seems hopeless, maintaining my focus on You. You've even given a promise of peace, if I can just keep my mind stayed on You. Even when I focus on staying focused, I still lose my focus. So hard, seems hopeless! When I wake, I remember that you woke me up and I'm most thankful! Devoting special, private time; meditation with You on my mind. Wish I could stay in that place, but so much to do, so little time! Reminded of traveling mercies, every time I'm driving, and a car gets too close to me. Reminded of patience, when road rage rises up in me. Making it to work on time, but vanity is my focus. Am I dressed to impress? Ooh, my hair is a mess! Throughout the workday, deadlines run through my mind. I'm getting behind! Tempted to take shortcuts. Reminded, in everything do as you're doing it for the Lord! The workday's done, wanting to have some fun. You should enjoy your youth, old age too and everything in the middle. Still reminded, I'll be held accountable, so be responsible! A day complete, time to rest your feet, lay your head. Dreams seem to take you wherever they want you to go. Impossible to focus in your sleep. Still, visions come through dreams, reminding of destiny. Rest and reflection at the end of the week. It still seems hopeless to maintain my focus on You, but it's becoming clear that Your Holy Spirit was always there, not only as a guarantee, not only to comfort me, but also to guide me, remind me to stay focused!

—Scripture References—
Isaiah 26:3, Ecclesiastes 11:9, Colossians 3:23, 2 Corinthians 1:3 and 4

A BATTLE LOST

Defiling the body! Waging war against my very own soul! Cast down, oh my soul! How can I do this to myself? Disappointed in another battle lost. Tossed my God aside for another joy ride! Now I'm more depressed than ever. As a man, I thought I had discipline because I said, "Never again!" Familiar sin keeps calling. Idle mind, twiddling fingers, hesitating, knowing I'm about to give in. Long life, a blessing, I was thinking as she was undressing. Need as much time as I can get to get back in right standing. "Turn out the light and come to bed," she said. (Shaking my head!)

—Scripture References—
Romans 6:19, 1 Corinthians 6:18, Proverbs 7:4–23

WHAT'S REAL

Why so downcast, oh my soul, though my hope already be in God? Temporary tribulations, trials and tests seem eternal! Temper at a boiling point, patience at an end! I bend over backwards to do things right and stand upright. Still bent, still broken. Cracking up, feel like I'm breaking down. I'm hurting so bad! Drowning in depression, sinking in despair! Making bad decisions for temporary relief. Intoxicated because I can't take the pain! The next morning feeling worse than before. When will I learn? Addiction won't let me go! The decision, no longer in my control. Lost my free will, now a slave to sin again! That's why I wear a frown. Cast down, oh my soul, though I still do hope in God. Just wish it wasn't so hard to stand upright. What was I meant to learn, why this fight? After years, decades of depression, one thing I have learned. Feelings are fickle, never to place your faith in, base your decisions on. Disciple doesn't give in to feelings, differing instant gratification for a grander prize. So now, instead of feelings being my guide, I have matured. There is a difference between how I feel and what's real. No matter the feeling, going to stay the course. Your Word is real, is truth, is life! I now fully realize! Learned my lesson, earned my stripes. Now in line to receive my prize!

—Scripture References—
Psalm 42 (entire chapter), Proverbs 2:7

HOLY GHOST PARTY

No party like a Holy Ghost party because a Holy Ghost party does not stop! Cut a rug, stomping! Spinning around, hopping up and down! Sing out loud from the bottom of your soul! Praise so hard that you lose control! If you have formal teaching or even taught yourself, it's time to get that instrument off the shelf! Gather with the band and play until you can play no more! This is a celebration, a Holy Ghost party, with heavenly hosts in attendance. In Christ, we have so much to celebrate and be grateful for! So beat them drums for the Lord! Blow those horns for the Lord! Rhythm and melody to get all the people on one accord. Harmony in celebration. Unity in the Lord! Holy Ghost party, all aboard!

—Scripture References—
Psalm 16:11, 96:11–13; Revelation 19:7–9

FINAL TEST

Tears of pain, sleepless nights! Struggles of the flesh, tearing at the fabric of my being! Losing this test. Fear struck, disturbed, hypnotic depression! Could there be meaning in all this? The enemy stole with a kiss. Stole so many things from me. Now he sent death for me at the lowest point in the valley. Failure after failure, my heart failing too! Trials and tribulations, suffering and affliction! Current condition, critical! Falling to pieces, reaching for a lifeline. I need some relief! Pain, pressure, and grief. Stored up, poured out, still full of things abominable to me, eroding my sanity! Pressure all around me! Pressure growing more and more! Exploding, imploding, erupting, melt down. Was so hot on fire. Getting cold now. So, so tired! Sound of a sigh. Time for my last breath. Life's come to an end. Flat line! Body breaking down, drying up. Returning to dust. Death, separation from the body. Spirit returning to the breath of life. Soul at rest. Peace at last. Still, quiet, nothingness. Then a sound, a call, a rise. All things made new! New life, new body, spiritually glorified. Seeing Him just as He is! Knowing Him just as I am known by Him. No more crying! Paradise, heaven, peace, and unity, the way it was supposed to be! Love, all encompassing! Joy continually! No more corruptibility! Not knowing sickness or disease. No more war, no more pain. Never knowing hunger again! Reflecting on life's journey on earth feels like just a moment in time. Was more than worth all the suffering, the sacrifice. Can't be compared with new abundant life, glory divine! Treasures never imagined, forever and ever! Rectified to Christ and the Father all at the same time!

—Scripture References—
John 10:10; Hebrews 9:27; Deuteronomy 7:19; James 1:2; 2 Peter 2:9; 1 Thessalonians 1:4; Psalm 78:39; 1 Peter 1:6 and 7, 4:12 and 13; Revelation 21 (entire chapter), 22 (entire chapter)

COURTROOM

As a prisoner captured, bound, and enslaved! I stand guilty. Charged with the shape that has formed me, that of iniquity. Before I came to know the light, I didn't even know I was in darkness—blacked out, blocked out, locked out! A breach, a gulf, a sea, dividing me from all I could not see. In darkness, carnal senses are honed, giving a glimmer, projecting shadows. Visibly, with some life, bodies here to do their time in the gallows, then fade, degrade back into the shallow dust. Though, just barely able to function, still blind, still bound for the sinking ground. My accuser is also the same one that has enslaved me. He had me tangled up in sin from the very beginning, then started professing the law, condemning with a death sentence! Now, I've seen it all! No chance for repentance, no opportunity for appeal. Who can appoint me a lawyer, how can I make a deal? At the appointed hour, the light shined from up on a hill, down on all the inhabitants, all the people. Descendant of Abraham, root of Jesse. Chosen by the Great I Am to represent me! Before He defends me, He begins to work in me and on me, so I can see things properly. Beginning with a spark, neurotransmitters fire throughout the brain, mapping plots, connecting dots, illuminating hearts and minds to the truth! Shackle and chain release, descend. Foundation solid, stable. The light of God's love has allowed me to see! The Truth, The Way, and The Life have set me free! The blood of deliverance pronounced innocence for a sinner such as me!

—Scripture References—
Lamentations 3:58; Jeremiah 51:36; Romans 5:8 and 9, 6:23; Proverbs 10:16; John 1:5, 8:32, 9:25; Ecclesiastes 3:20; 2 Samuel 22:32 and 47

PECULIAR THINGS

Time, a peculiar thing. What are the chances, in all of time, that I'm alive presently? When my light goes out, will time cease for me? When I rise to new life, will it be instantaneously? The concept of before and after, very peculiar, when considering beginnings and endings. If there was a beginning, and there will be an end, what happened before the beginning of time and what happens after the end? This rhyme is not a riddle, just a little peculiar as I attempt to comprehend these things. Like what does "now" even mean? Peculiar how the largest forms in the universe resemble the most minute. Solar systems with planetary rotations and revolutions. Atoms with protons and neutrons. Everything relative and made up of the same thing. Amazing, when you consider it all. Peculiar how we control things we don't fully understand. Utilizing invisible waves to travel at speeds that make transmission almost instantaneous. Harnessing energies so great they could obliterate the whole world. Are we really in control, or have we started the ball rolling and now impossible to regain a hold? Just thought I would mention, man-made inventions are doomed to become idols, whenever they replace people's focus on God's creation. Peculiar how man's accomplishments make him think he no longer depends on God. Trust in God replaced. Has become placed solely on men. But God was not created for us, we were created for Him. Why then do we think we've risen, in society, when great has been our fall? Many peculiar things I've seen in this foreign land. The most peculiar of them all, I would have to say is man.

—Scripture References—
1 Peter 2:7–10, Romans 1:28–32

ART OF WAR

Age old, art of war. Three-fold destruction/discord. The Modus Operandi of the father of lies. The devil steals, kills and destroys. As an object that envies humanity, this brings him much joy. He will steal the truth from you, before the blink of an eye. But he has not only stolen the truth, but replaced it with a lie, sowing seeds of discord in your psyche. Replacing love with anxiety, stress and worry. All derivations of fear. Implanting the very thing to bring about the destruction of everything around you, all that God has given. Once he's stolen and destroyed everything in your life, he'll send death to come claim his prize. Stress kills, but perfect love casts out fear. So why do you think you're still walking in love when worry and stress has taken control of your thought process? Worrying comes from thinking everything hinges on you. Leaving out God, total rejection of faith! Where is the trust? He has you and working everything together for your good? That's what love would have told you, the very thing the devil stole. Now you're walking around like you're on your own, everything spiraling out of control. Use the Word of God to get back what the devil stole. Systematically cast down every proud and lofty lie the devil tries to make you believe! Replace it with the Word of Truth. The Word that should already be engrafted in your heart. Having the mind of Christ, every thought in line with Him. Never forget who you are, who you belong to and what you're fighting for! Age old, art of war.

—Scripture References—
John 8:44, 10:7–10 and 18:36, 2 Timothy 2:1–4, Matthew 6:25–34, Revelation 12:10–17, 2 Corinthians 10:4 and 5

51

DREAMS

Glimmer little light. While things in this life seem what dreams are made of, still, dimmer is this light, the farther I am from You. Majestic, memorable moments mean nothing without You. Must shine bright to show others the way to the true light. Things in this life that seem like dreams pale in comparison to Heaven! 'Til He appears, through the day or by night, beams of light shining from within for the sake of men, but I set my dreams on Him.

—Scripture References—
Joel 2:28, Matthew 5:14–16

52

WARRIOR UNSTOPPABLE

Warrior unstoppable! Slay a thousand Dragons with a single blow! Don't they know my Father, the Almighty? Standing around, arms crossed like they are the boss. Pity, pity little things, bringing wrath upon them from the King of kings. Given to me, power to devour the enemy! Singing songs of victory, for the war already won. Satan's spawn upon the earth, releasing seed for increase, to consume the earth. Many battles won, taking total control for a time. So many people lost their soul following the masses! Pity, pity little things, bringing wrath upon you from The King of kings. I fight for those chosen few. Hear and answer the battle call. Warrior unstoppable!

—Scripture References—
Joshua 23:10, Matthew 22:14, Revelation 19:16

SIMPLICITY

Remembering the times when it was all so easy. Never had a worry or regret. Simplicity, we met and got along great! But now, it's complicated. Often finding myself most agitated. Juggling the cares of this life—responsibilities, obligations, worries, temptations, tests, trials, and tribulations! Whew, so much to do, so much being done to me! Will I continue to stand or sink back into the sins of man? My heart doesn't trust me, but God knows me and my heart. My path is often shaky, but God knew it from the start. When I enter my darkest hour, for I fret I have not seen it yet, God, Holy Ghost power and grace, will let me get to the end of my race! Then, at last, no more tests. Just simplicity again at its best!

—Scripture References—
Mark 4:19, 1 John 3:20, 2 Corinthians 1:12, John 10:10

PAIN AND PURPOSE

Mundane, life's pursuits when they bear no spiritual fruits. Pain and purpose, dichotomous yet synonymous. In life, everyone's looking for pleasure and gain, but the passion of the Christ entails misery and strife. Shallow appearance often takes precedence over quintessence. All too true, the mask we wear. Dolling up the face, manipulating hair. Dare I say, the closest people to you don't know you. Reveal the truth behind the veil. As we travail along our journey, regression propels progression. To learn, sometimes unlearning must be done, assimilating lies throughout life. Reprove God's truths in the light. Revise your priorities. Brokenness into beauty, sifting through the fragments of pain. Jesus Christ evident as God puts the pieces together again. Many facets of beauty you see when facing a new creation. Inner beauty shining thru. The pain that built character in you. Now we finally see that all else is vanity.

—Scripture References—
Ecclesiastes (entire book); 2 Thessalonians 2:13; Colossians 1:24; 2 Corinthians 3:14–16, 5:17; Ephesians 5:13; Leviticus 15:12; Jeremiah 18:6; Romans 9:21

EYES

Eyes, said to be the windows to your soul, giving a viewpoint in the earth. Physical images and perceptions attained without physical contact. Taken for granted, the power of the eye that is never satisfied. Able to take all attention away from the spiritual, focusing only on the carnal. Within the five senses it's never been explained how you can feel when someone's looking at you. Stare at a lady's derriere and she'll begin to pull her shirt down. Someone looking at you will cause you to look around, 'til your eyes meet. mysterious the eye, but more dangerous still. Able to gain control and guide all your members, by bringing carnal images to the brain, where the battle begins, causing carnal contemplations and meditations. Next thing you know, your tongue gets to talking or your feet get to walking or your hands get to grabbing for things it should not. Carnal eyes that are never satisfied, only sink you back into carnal sin and degradation. The eye only interested in what pleases self. I'd rather gouge out an eye than be a slave to sin 'til I die! What can I do to counteract the attack of my own carnal members? There is another eye that we have access to. This third eye is spiritual. With the aid of The Word and the Holy Spirit, illumination is given into the things of heaven and a guide; how to be rectified. This spiritual eye gives a spiritual path laid out by Grace, when walking by faith. To finish this race, the carnal eyes must be denied, not looking to the left or right. Keep your focus straight ahead and heed the Word of God, the light and lamp to The Way, The Truth and life. Let His Spirit lead you, and when you pray, seeking to reach the Heavenlies, close those carnal eyes!

—Scripture References—
Matthew 6:22 and 23, 7:3–5, Acts 26:16–18, Ephesians 1:18, Luke 11:34, Mark 9:4

NOW

Now is the time to bow, take a knee! Give honor to the King of kings. Confess Jesus Christ as Lord. Now is the time to serve, take a knee! Let Him rise in you. By Him you are implored. Accomplish great feats, make demons flee, perform great works, do the impossible! Now is the time, while it's still called now. In the fullness of time when all will be resurrected, even those who pierced Jesus will see Him coming in the clouds. They all will bow, but if I were you, I'd take a knee now!

—Scripture References—
Philippians 2:9–11, 1 Corinthians 1:7, 1 Thessalonians 3:13, 4:13–18, 5:1–11, 2 Thessalonians 2(entire chapter), Revelation 1:7

SAY HIGH

Say high, say high, say HIGH! Fly on wings to the Most High! When all the good work is done, time for a transformation. All creation has been waiting to see us revealed. Still a mystery what we'll be, a veil until we reach our appointed destination. Meeting The Husband man, flying high in the sky. The One who's veil has already been unveiled, now seeing Him as he really is. With eyes incorruptible and a body glorified, we will actually be like God! Can't fathom things so high, above my imagination. I just can't wait to fly so high in the sky, the body of Christ on one accord, to meet The Lord! So high, most high, say HIGH!

—Scripture References—
Romans 8:22–25, 1 Corinthians 13:12 and 13, 15:50–54, 2 Corinthians 3:16,18,
1 Thessalonians 4:15–18

A BREATH

Though my life be but a breath, I will use it to worship You! From now on, until my dying breath, allow me to express my gratitude! You breathed into me the breath of life. Your breath is my life. May it be multiplied, as I offer it back to You. Unfortunately, now that it's with me, in the land of iniquity, it's been contaminated. Foul mouth, foul language, foul odors proliferated! The stench of death upon my breath, as I devour life to maintain my own. Still, may my every utterance be received by You, through the cleansing blood, a sweet aroma in Your nostril. However off key, may my life song be a pleasing sound in Your ear. No time to waste on trivial pursuits. Let everything I pursue bring glory to You! Though my life be but a breath, as it dissipates to nothingness, may You redeem all that is true.

—Scripture References—
Genesis 2:7, James 3:9, 2 Timothy 1:6–8, Philippians 1:20 and 21

THE ACCUSER

Adoration will be given, we know where it goes. One appointed above all, to usher in God's Glory in Heaven. Himself, made glorious to the heavenly eye. Still, a liar from the start, opposer from the heart. Created to tear apart, factions in heaven. Not wanting to give, desires only to steal. Why ever appointed at all? Seems to have been the worst choice. War in heaven! No more adoration, replaced with covetousness and deceit. The audacity to think he could overthrow the Almighty! No match for the Lord, cast down in defeat. His position now, changed. Never meant to maintain it anyway. Still, for a short time, able to approach the throne. No longer for adoration, position now, accusations. Both day and night, accusing God's own! Conversations, God and Satan. "Devil, ever considered my servant Job? Upright, even perfect in my sight. Yeah-yeah but remove that hedge and I'll have him curse you before the end of the night. God, all your creation has become an abomination to You! They worship me, money, their god is their belly! All they want is what they see! How could you ever consider them replacing me? Point me to all You call upright, remove their hedge, and I'll have them cursing You by the end of the night!" When trials come, remember these conversations. The devil, day and night talking to God, no longer for adoration but accusations, accusing you! During your test, it is not the time to throw in the towel. Don't give Satan that satisfaction! Just approach God's throne day and night, with love and adoration and drown out the enemy's accusations!

—Scripture References—
John 8:44–47, Revelation 12:10–12, 1 Peter 5:8, Job 1:6–12

STREET LIFE

Click clack, strapped for battle fighting for territory! Street life, a dot on the map, beef on your block because they walked across the wrong corner! Smoking gun, blood on the pavement. Live by the sword, kill and be killed, your reward.

Tick tock, times up! Fast life, early death, by twenty-five either dead or in jail. Serving twenty-five to life, final sentence, final residence to get your mail!

Hip hop, gangster music, trap rap stands, glorifying street life! Turning children to the streets for their education, hard lessons learned. Falling for the tricks, falling in the trap, that's why they call it trap rap. Cold hard streets beat the best, defeat the rest. Destroys every boy trying to be that man! And here stand our children's role models, rappers given a gift to leave the streets, but still promote it glorify it, have so many dying on It. With the pen they write, with the words they speak so much blood is on their hands. The lust of money sex and drugs, street life provides for all the thugs.

Hard drugs heroine, or whatever be the latest drug trend. Sippin' lean, methamphetamines, ecstasy, or molly poppin'. Sending you on your favorite trip high as a rocket ship, but when you come down, you're lower than before. So, you search for that same high that made you soar! Selling everything to get more, been sold your soul. Would do anything for just one more hit! Lower than you ever thought you could go, all because you wanted to get high! Users and abusers, dealers and distributors, gangsters and hustlers, pimps and hoes. Whatever the street gives it surely takes more. That's all the street knows.

—Scripture References—
Matthew 26:52, James 3:3–12, 2 Timothy 2:22, 2 Peter 3:3–7, 1 Peter 4:3

THE HILLS

I set my eyes unto the hills, from which cometh my help! That's the farthest I can see, waiting for Him to return to me. I close my eyes, to my surprise, He's already here, my comfort, my guide. God is Spirit, is to be adored in spirit, in truth. Carnal eyes will never know God, only proximal images. Still, hills and meadows reveal His awesome power, show His divinity. He could possibly be just over the hill, in a cloud, coming for His glorified body! That's why I still look to the hills, even though I feel Him inside me. One day truly rectified, my soul yearns insatiably! Daydreaming, vague stare, there but not there. Unaware my spirit has carried me away. Still can't quite get to where I need to be, the place The One to truly set me free. Dropped back down to reality, in this carnal body, but to me this is not what is real. That's why I continue to look to the hills, even though God be Spiritual and I carnal. Even with my carnal eyes, even though they fail me, one thing I've come to realize. When my help comes, He causes me to rise with glorified eyes, to see Him just as He really is!

—Scripture References—
Psalm 121:1 and 2, John 14:26, Hebrews 10:37

LOST AND FOUND

Am I winning or losing? Lost so much. Some, time done stole! The more things in life I try to control, the more I lose. Lost my innocence, lost my virginity. Found so many lovers. Also found an STD. Got rid of that, thank God! Many women lost and found. Try to keep one around. Lost and found many friends. Some still here, sticking in. When I lost certain family and loved ones to death, felt like I lost a part of myself! Found a home, lost a house. Left my parents, found a spouse. Forged a family of my own. Lost that too! Lost wealth, my looks, lost my health. Starting to feel like I've lost it all! Am I winning or losing? Neglected to mention, wanted to save the best for last. I found the Lord! I'm so thankful He found me! Found out that I was lost. Though God gives and takes away, He saves the best for last! Past sins erased, cleansed from head to toe! Preparing you for transition. Last thing lost on earth, life itself, or so it seems. A new beginning brings new life. More abundant, much more profound, I've found! All I see, beyond my imagination, still a surprise. One thing, though. I now know. I AM WINNING!

—Scripture References—
Job 1:21, Matthew 6:19–21, 1 John 2:2 and 3:1–3, 1 Peter 2:25, Philippians 3:21

TRUTH

Truth, you seek, truth you find. Nothing more divine! Uncompromising, unadulterated, uncontaminated! Fact, not an opinion to be debated. Though debate it they do, still. Truth- what is, lie- what is not. Choice- what is in free will. Discernment reveals truth, resounding from within. To know truth, experience teaches, or already self-evident. Knowledge in truth, sets free chains of bondage, previously entangled by lies and sin. Strategic lies, false facts, compromise. Those are the devil's attacks. Though many will fall, Truth will stand tall above all! Created for the purpose of glorifying the True and living God! Lies just glorify the fraud. Many stories unfold throughout history. The great story told started out as a mystery. Messiah unveiled; the Truth revealed. Salvation, restoration, sanctification, healed, resurrected, manifold manifest, blessed! The realest thing ever written. Take hold of Truth, not opinion. Fact not fiction!

—Scripture References—
John 14:6, 1 Corinthians 1:20–25 and 3:19

RIGHTEOUS PRAYERS

Intercessor, prayer warrior! Such a power at work within. Creating a porthole, releasing supernaturally from the heavenly to earth. Much avails the righteous prayers in total submission to Your will. Your Spirit reels and reveals, performing all Your Word. No void, divine purpose will be accomplished! Complete and total surrender, rendering this tabernacle a vessel for spiritual warfare. Time to pray, get out of the way and see the Lord cut to pieces all the snares of the enemy! Provision for every need! Direction for destiny! Protection for family! Victory, victory, victory!

—Scripture References—
James 5:16, Romans 8:26 and 27, Ephesians 6:20, Job 16:19–21, Psalm 5:11, Philippians 1:19, John 15:26, 1 John 5:4, 1 Corinthians 15:7

ARISE

The clock strikes twelve, just when the last piece of bread is cleared off the shelf. All the provisions are gone! Time to lay down and die! Desperation sinks down to the bottom of your belly where that last piece of bread lies. Despair, lost all hope, no longer can cope. Just so tired of the struggle! Close eyes. Arise at the dawning of a new day! New mercies, provision anew, another chance at repentance! When the clock struck twelve, when you cleared the last piece of bread off the shelf, you cleared away all past regrets! You hear, as if it were someone whispering in your ear, rise to the dawning of a New Year! Every day a blessing, a new year, a monumental milestone! When the clock strikes twelve, no need to mourn the clearing out of your shelves. Just close your eyes and rise to the dawning of a new day! With Jesus Christ in control of your life, the impossible becomes mere child's play. The things He can do in a day. All things made new!

—Scripture References—
1 Kings 17:10–16, Matthew 28:1–6, Revelation 21:5

VANITY

So much lost, so much forgotten. They rust, they fade, turn rotten. Material gains so vain. Family, friends, loved ones come and go. Past generations we don't even know. All good things come from God, but to lose them again can be so hard. The Lord does give, does take away, every moment of every day. Discouraging life's journey through the valley of the shadows of death. Since I can't take it with me, all is vanity. But God can use me for His glory. He can beautify this story. What seemed all wrong somehow turns out right. Redeeming all creation through all history. Restore all generations in divine restoration. This was why it was all meant to be, but you won't see it if your focus is on vanity.

—Scripture References—
Matthew 6:19 and 20, Job 1:21, Psalm 23:4 and 6, Ecclesiastes 9:5, Revelation 21:1–5

DECEIVED

I heard of a redeemer with a crown of Glory to share. If not for sin, I would have rushed in. Became a believer and took up my cross to bear. If you want to win you have to help carry the burden. I learned of the deceiver, blurring lines, casting shadows. A liar from the beginning. Oh, how I've been deceived! Though saved, still carnal, mentally contaminated with so many lies assimilated through time! I'm a believer in the redeemer, but the deceiver has caused me to be a receiver of lies along with the truth! More confusion still, figuring the difference between what you feel and what's real. Raised in iniquity, sin shaped my priorities. I believed in love, but love was not what I thought, deceived! I received a dream that was given to me, bought into it wholeheartedly, deceived! I achieved many victories, but was fighting the wrong fight, deceived! Fought hard for what I felt but not for what's right, learned feelings are fickle, deceived! Thought if I followed my heart, it would bring me where I should be, deceived! Leaning to my understanding, thought that would lead me in the right direction, but left with a destination of death! Deceived because I was lost in a world deceived. Fortunately, The Truth found me and set me free! Bless the Lord God Almighty! Still, guard your heart and test your thoughts. Even though the Truth you have received, never think you're above being deceived.

—Scripture References—
Matthew 16:24, 1 Corinthians 3:3, John 8:32, Revelation 12:9, Acts 7:35, Proverbs 3:5 and 6

AFROCENTRIC

Afrocentric, pro black, fist raised! Black pride, black beauty, black rights. Been to the bottom, been sold as a slave! Been oppressed by "the man." Still standing, stronger than ever, though the enemy did plan our demise. Opposite sides of the spectrum create antagonism. Propaganda made to make white right, black wrong. White pure, black dirty. Black weak, white strong. Black dumb, white witty. White beauty, black ugly. Even invented\innovated a lily-white messiah, making salvation seem to come from the Caucasian bloodline. Whitewashing the bible to continue to oppress the black people through colonization. So much wrong done to the African American. Taken from their land. Lost their identity, lost their name. Confused, disillusioned, but not ashamed. Every fight, every struggle, to gain back what's been stolen by "the man." I hear a resounding whisper in the wind, "Revolution!" Tired of being under the man's thumb! Just when it seems dreams of equality, peace and harmony are achieved, knocked back down again! Revolution seems to be the only solution for the Afrocentric, African American. But now I am a new creation. Here I stand Christian! Found my identity in the almighty! Above any race, I am a Christian. The entire human race can get a foretaste of glory divine and can be saved because of Jesus' sacrifice! Salvation for the lost, that is our fight! Walking in righteousness, that is our fight! Walking in love, in peace even toward our enemy, knowing the Lord fights my battles for me! Revelation teaches me revolution will come at the second coming of Jesus the Christ! While waiting for that day, currently need to make ourselves ready. Follow closely end times prophecy and instructions for His people. In the end, "the man" will not stand. Not talking about Caucasian, but Satan! The plan has always come from a demonic entity, carried out by secret societies. Secret plans, subliminal attacks, subtle deceit. Do you know your true enemy? Afrocentric, African American, make sure you're a part of the right revolution!

—Scripture References—
2 Corinthians 5:16–21

LOVE

Finding love in a world so cold. Coming up short, this is getting old! Love is kind; love is sweet. Love is patient, making all things complete. I Saw a thing that looked like love. Love conquers all, standing ten feet tall! Had a dream about it but woke up without it. Love always gives. Love, why we live. Love above anything! Love, the reason why we sing. Love practically, love factually, love actually. Love, love, l-o-v-e! Just when I gave up on love, Love found me!

—Scripture References—
Romans 8:39, 1 Corinthians 13:1–8, 1 John 4:8 and 16

ABOVE EVERYTHING

Difficult roads often lead to beautiful destinations, though the road less traveled is narrow. Few know, many in the beginning, but who will see the end destination? Once on the right road, don't even dare look back! Just learn everything you need to gain along the journey. Maintain through all affliction and pain. Learn the most essential lesson. Love above everything!

—Scripture References—
Matthew 7:13

DEATH'S STING

The sting of death at soul's last breath, when all is done with nothing left. Fearful anticipation, apprehension of this solemn day, when the body, so cherished, begins to decay. All other thoughts paltry, insignificant, after a taste, staring death in the face. Looming in your heart, luminous! Every day is one day closer to meeting that great opposer. Opposing progression, wanting to keep moving but stopped dead in your tracks! Time, ever fleeting, leaving, no sense in chasing. Such a travesty, wasting. Tick-tock, when the clock stops, can't go back or forward. Sin's grasp has locked you tight in death's grip! What was the point of life at all! Nothing to something, back to nothing! The point of it all becomes apparent on the day of the great call. The One that gives every good thing has another gift to bring. He calls you to a new life, more abundantly! Just when you thought you were done, Jesus stared death in the face and won! He has the keys, now, to death and the grave! All power in His hands in control of everything! Now, death, where is your sting!

—Scripture References—
1 Corinthians 15:55, Revelation 1:18, Ecclesiastes 9:5

JOB INTERVIEW

Why are there those that seek after my soul to destroy it? Slippery, slithering, slick, quick to rob of eternity, replacing with current iniquity. Want my words to always be carnal, worldly. My meditations lustful, fleshly. Keeping me away from my destiny. Showing my Creator, I'm not worthy. Setting traps to destroy me! If God loves me, how can He allow this to be? The enemy in heaven, the archangel Lucifer, in charge of praise and worship unto the Lord. Now Satan, cast down to the earth, his destiny, the sulfur lake, burning for all eternity! A short time he has to drag as many as he can down to hell with him. Consider this in your analysis. Who better to interview and scrutinize for a position than the previous person employed? Now, we have the honor and privilege in charge of praise and worship unto the Lord! Mind you, this position is provisional. Your probationary period is your opportunity to shine, period! You can prove your enemy right, curse God, and die! Blame Him for your every problem. Or you can endure to the end serving Him with submission in love. As free will has been given, choose you today, whom you shall serve! I'd rather serve the One that created me, that has thoughts for my good, than a proven enemy that would destroy me if he could. If not for the Lord on my side, His word that said, "Touch not my anointed!" The One that sent His Son who already won the battle for us and showed us how it should be done!

—Scripture References—
Job 1 and 2(entire chapters); Revelation 12:10–12, 20:10; 1 Samuel 24:6; Jeremiah 29:11; Psalm 40:14

STIR IT UP

Stir up the gift, store up treasures. Eternal rewards beyond measure. Stewardship dictates this gift is not just for you. Have to multiply, causing blessings to overflow and continue to flow accomplishing everything ordained by the King of kings. One body bound together by one Spirit. Each member does their part. One faith, one God, one Son. God head and body. Individually, I can't do anything. Working together under the direction of Headship, we can accomplish all we were created for! Specific gifts given for specific assignment. No time should be spent on envy. What God has for you is for you. Focus on what you need to do! Stir up the gift, store up treasures. Keep your eyes on the prize.

—Scripture References—
2 Timothy 1:6, Matthew 6:19–21, Philippians 4:13

REDEEMED

Stuck in this degenerating condition of addiction! The enemy cultivates my destruction. God still works in His divine will to fulfill plans for my good. Through all my bad He's still sustaining me. All the chances I had to get it right, He's still making a way for me! God of love, Your mercies they fail not! You endure in patience when I would have given up on myself. Blessed assurance has kept me in this fight. My weakness and infirmities remind me of Your Sovereignty. Day by day, hour by hour my strength is sustained in Your mercies. Your strength is unto righteousness as You stand and fight my battles for me! Only You know, from whence I came. Only You know where You want me to go. You prepare a banquet celebration, inauguration in the presence of my enemies. You knew beforehand and laid Your Grace along the path of my failures, so I would last and pass the test with flying colors. Goodness and mercy follow behind me to clean and clear my trail. Every missed step erased. No sin to be identified, not even a trace. You are so great, words fail me! Holy Spirit, allow your intercessions to avail my prayers, Jesus my High Priest. I just can't do you justice. Your righteousness I cannot fathom! How can they deny You? Random conversations about conditions in the nation, leaving You out of the equation, or worse still, blaming You for our every sin and consequence therein. I just mind my business, try to block out the noise. God of heaven, just wish they knew You like I do. How long do I have to abide with these wicked people? Just then, I'm reminded of my own grievous sins and how you accept me back time and time again. Have to learn better, in humility. Your love and patient endurance. Remembering Your mercy to me. I must do more for my brother. We are all stuck in this degenerative addictive condition of sin, all causing us to stand condemned. If not for the One who knew no sin and loved us before we knew what love was. I stand in humility, a sinner supreme. No better than any other. Just blessed by Grace to be redeemed!

—Scripture References—
Lamentations 3:22 and 23, Psalm 92:5, Romans 8:26, 1 John 2:12

FAVOR

Savor the flavor of divine favor! It's been placed over you, nothing more beautiful. So sweet to know the Lord sees me as special! Gleaming in the eye of the Almighty! He accepts you as His child. Nothing you can pay for, nothing you deserve. God's unmerited favor, founded on purpose, in love to accomplish all you could not do alone. Favor put you in your position. Favor linked you up with the right people. Favor kept you from the wrong people. Now you're connected, in place, the platform made. Now is your time to shine! Favor brought you here to perform what you were created for. Treasures deposited in you, gifts too, made room for you to mix it up and pour it out. Returning to you only to stir it up and release it again. That's what a vessel does. It's been given so that you can multiply. The vessel is not the treasure, but what's inside. God's placed treasures in earthen vessels and gave gifts to men, but not solely for self. Don't let your pride get it twisted. In humility, we have the ability to savor the sweet flavor of God's unmerited favor!

—Scripture References—
Luke 4:18 and 19, 2 Corinthians 4:7, Psalm 34:8

MIND OF CHRIST

The mind of Christ says die to self in this life. Realize this life is not the prize. Focus your eyes higher than your belly. Readiness in sacrifice prepares you to reap heavenly rewards. True blessedness is not temporal but meant to be eternally enjoyed. You're blessed to be poor in finance and in spirit too because you're rich in faith, reaping joy unspeakable! Blessed to be persecuted for righteousness' sake because that will make you great in the Kingdom of heaven. Blessed when you're reviled, blessed when you're rejected. You were meant to be set apart; by Him, you are accepted. Blessed when you give to men because you're lending to the Lord. Blessed when treasures have been taken by Satan. In the end, you will recover all and more if you endure. Rejected by the world because you're not of this world. Remember this, when settling here, into your career, home, family and community, don't get too comfortable. We're just pilgrims passing through!

—Scripture References—
1 Corinthians 2:16, Matthew 5:3–12, James 2:5, Psalm 4:3, Hebrew 11:13, Philippians 3:19

CHOSEN PATH

Who I am - even a mystery to me. Surely not the sum parts of my molecular body. Strangely, mysteriously God chose to allow that to remain a mystery to me. Along the chosen path, clues laid progress made. Understanding more about who I am and what I'm here for. Still not seeing clearly, spiritually what I will be. Walking by faith on the chosen path we call destiny. Starting out, destiny sounds so exciting, an adventure so inviting. Along the chosen path, chosen trials as you take up your cross and bear its pain. Destiny doesn't seem so good to me anymore. Guess that's why it had to be a mystery. Mysterious still what we shall be. Along the chosen path, as I grasp to attain knowledge of who I am, I learn it's not about me. The Sun doesn't revolve around the earth, the earth does not revolve around me. My worth can only be found finding my place in a greater body. Along the chosen path I learn my gifts given for God's glory, to be shared freely for the up building of His Kingdom and edification of the body of Christ. Destiny is looking good again in this new body, even though it's still a mystery, spiritually what I will be throughout all eternity. Along the chosen path as you bear your cross, you realize so many things temporal are really what's weighing you down. As you understand their eternal insignificance you lay them down. Things you thought were important now not worthy at all to block and stop you from your Destiny! Along the chosen path, picking up jewels of wisdom clues to your identity, you embrace your changes and reach an epiphany! I am transformation! Changes not solely occurring in my temporal body but I'm growing and changing spiritually! Still can't see clearly what I will be, but I learned that I will be like God, finally able to really and truly see Him! Transformed into the likeness of Jesus, joining the family of Almighty God! That's bigger than believing the earth revolves around me! Still, along the chosen path I've learned humility. The Grace of God, God's gift given freely. If you can't relate at all to what I've found on the chosen path, you're on the wrong road!

—Scripture References—
1 Corinthians 15:42–56, Matthew 16:24–27, 1 John 3:1–3, 2 Corinthians 5:6–10

FISHERMAN

Fisher of men. Drowning, sinking. Ocean of sin. Bubbles, waves, commotion creating. Pulling down, one upon another. Frantic desperation, self-preservation. Attempting to rise but continuing indecent in descent. Bloody water makes it murky. Screams, "Lord, have mercy!" Sharks circling, feeding frenzy! Seems screams all in vain. Hold on, wait...Rescue team on duty! Lifeguard, life raft, lifesaver, lifeline. Arriving on the scene right on time! Diving deep down murky depths. Sacrificing self to save! Men under too long. Appearing in the shadows, death! No pulse left! He breathes into you, His breath. Arise, new life! Fisher of men goes away. Leaves lifeline and lifesaver behind. Keeping afloat, with hope, though the seas be foreign. Rise high, the crushing waves! Often devastated, but death abated. Still, rising above all. Waiting until the rescue team returns again. Meanwhile, since in this ocean of sin, making sure new life is perpetuated, you become a fisher of men!

—Scripture References—
Matthew 4:19, 24:14; Romans 3:25, 6:10; Psalm 23:4, 123:3; 2 Corinthians 4:8–12

LOW PLACE

I despise the shame! Sin's seduction made me to blame! Not nearly what I should be, as aspiration's perspiration puff up only to go back into deflation, total evaporation! Placed in humility, I've been denied the fame. God knows, no profit in it if I lose my soul, which led me into digression. I despise the shame of being an alien in a foreign land ruled by an enemy that wants to devour my mind, soul and body! So many blind eyes only seeing lies. Despised for standing for Truth. Standing up, standing out on The Rock while so many sink in sand. Set apart, in this foreign land even from some of my family and friends. I despise the earth, this perverse generation! Where is my King! He despised the shame that this life brings too, even being without sin, but when He returns again, He'll put everything back in right standing. For now, sin shapes the landscape and everything's looking dreary! Even some Christians on the platform water down their ministries with self-centered testimonies about prosperity. I don't fit in with them, definitely don't fit in with the world's theologies. Where do I fit in, in this world of sin? I have love for my brother, but despise the evil men do, my evil included too. Repugnant filth I'm attached to! I despise it, I tell you! Durability necessary, enduring the duration of a detestable existence, hell bent and malicious! Just when weariness almost drags me down beneath the ground, I'm reminded to pause from looking around. A higher plain need be attained to gain a renewed mind. Looking up, my faith restored, strength too. Sending praises up, heaven rains blessings down on me. Preparing me, in destiny! Use this broken thing to make a difference in the world for Your Kingdom up-building. Let not my pain be in vain! Transform every despicable syllable in my story to that of good. Good works, good fruits, good God that gets all the Glory! That's how He said it will be in the end, in the everlasting. That's why He told me not to worry.

—Scripture References—
Psalm 23:4, Mark 8:36 and 13:13, Ephesians 1:3

WHY THE DEVIL A LIE?

Why devil, lie devil? Gas on the pedal, speeding down the road of life. Words, meanings, intentions, and decisions, leading you in a certain direction. But where are you? Where are you headed? Often not knowing, moving in the wrong direction led by lies and false perceptions. What should I follow? What will take me where I need to go? Selfish ambition, money chasing, self-exalting? No! Though it may seem right, wrong direction, bro! You go to college, gain worldly knowledge, now you're ready for life. But knowledge puffs up, making you appear more than you are. Don't think so highly of yourself. Though worldly knowledge is gained, your brain is still saturated with lies and false perceptions, leading you in the wrong direction. Some people gain enough worldly knowledge to dare to call it God! Puffing up themselves as God! Correct wisdom teaches humility; in a vast universe, not even a smidgen you be. Can't look at a creation without acknowledging The Creator, and what we're here for. The fear of the Lord, the beginning of true knowledge. Why? Going back to those lies. False perceptions, leading you in the wrong direction, causing you to stand in a position in opposition to the One who created you! Standing beside the father of lies with the same sentence as the devil, pronounced to be evil! How I have been a fool! Now, trying to reconcile previous knowledge with new truth attained. Intense struggles in the brain! Lies want to stay, but they must go because you know better now. Clouds of deception clear; now the truth can be revealed! Clearly, now, can see. Why the devil a lie? An enemy that tried to keep you from the Truth, the Way, and the Life!

—Scripture References—
Proverbs 8:13, 9:10, 16:25; Job 28:28; 1 Corinthians 8:1; 2 Corinthians 5:11; John 8:44, 14:6; Ephesians 2:3; Romans 12:3

HAVE I EVER TOLD YOU?

Have I ever told You that I love You? The best thing that ever happened to me. Oh, how I wish that I could hold You. Be with You all the day, continually. Have I ever told you that I miss you? Never a day without You; I would ever want to see. Know that I always think about You. One true desire to be in Your family. Have I ever told You that I'm thankful? You've done it all; I do applaud You gratefully. Grow in You more and more. Adore You for what You do for in and through me. Have I ever told You that I praise You? Your biggest fan, I clap my hands, dancing and jumping, for You. Show You just what You mean to me. Have I ever told You that I never get tired of telling You all the things I've told You and more? Every time is like the first time for me. Though You gave me the gift of tongues, ten million wouldn't be enough to begin to tell You! Have I ever told You?

—Scripture References—
Mark 12:30, 1 Corinthians 12:1–11, Hebrews 13:15, Romans 8:16, 1 John 3:1

TIDES

Tides rise and resend. Waves roll and rush in. Ride a wave for the mere joy, catching it as it begins, knowing that joy has an end. The greater the wave, the greater the joy, the greater the crash! Nothing in this life lasts. Sandcastles built only to come tumbling down with one great splash! Tides come in and then disappear as though they were never there. Tides turn from generation to generation, when care given is now taken. Grew strong through each passing wave, but before long, grew old with nothing left to hold onto. Holding on to something fluid is impossible. Hanging onto the sand always moving into the drag of the sea. Rushing in and dragging out, taking away the tangible. So much given, so much gone. Finally, your tide comes in. Change - the only constant, you see, as even you are dragged into the depth of the dead sea. Life, but a vapor. Every day must be savored, every love celebrated. While linear timelines have a beginning and an end, life is perpetuated in cycles. What you thought was the end is actually a new beginning, the latter much greater than the former. From the depths of the sea, bubbles begin to release. As mist rises and returns to a purer form, one last ride, but no crash. The corruptible laid down, the spirit returns to The Creator. Transformation taken, incorruptible and unshakable! No more tides, no more strife. Nothing can ever be taken again. You've finally arrived in everlasting life!

—Scripture References—
1 Corinthians 15:51–54, Psalm 42:7, Ephesians 4:14

JEWELS OF THE KINGDOM

I used to think I was poor until I saw a man eating from the trash can, with bare feet, sleeping on the concrete! Never experienced no food to eat, but always been hungry for more. By faith, I saw blue sapphire stone sitting at the floor of the throne. Learned in a classroom that humility is the key, but only life lessons teach true humility. There was One who humbled Himself as a servant, even to wash my feet! Pure gold lay on the ark of the covenant, streets of gold clear as pure glass! Never seen a wild thing feeling sorry for itself. A, so called, civilized society is where sin abides! Not only needs but storing up selfish desires on the shelf. Each gate, one great pearl! I thought I knew a lot until I met a man who knew infinity. The universal language, mathematics, God's fingerprint I see. Walking by faith and not sight. Laying out the inner and outer sanctuaries, mansions in Heaven. Even when I go wrong, it turns out right! Learned and gained and lost until it has all become a conundrum. Coming to completion, arriving at the perfect number seven. By faith I see the jewels of the Kingdom, not to be acquired, but to become one!

—Scripture References—
John 13:3–17, Revelation 10:7, 11:15, 21:9–27

HYMNS

Hmmm, hmmm, hmmm, hmmm, hmmm (humming melodiously)! Hymns of praise rise to lay at Your feet. Song and dance melodiously integrated into the beat. Instruments in harmony intensify, word personified! Heart and soul expressions spiritually reaching the heavens. Connections made, man and God. Creation production in accordance with the will of the Creator. These things, predestined, professing praise and worship with exaltation and magnification. Building up Your kingdom, telling Your story. All things done for Your Glory, for You are worthy!

—Scripture References—
Colossians 3:16, Ephesians 5:19, Nehemiah 12:46, Hebrews 2:12, Revelation 4:11

SELF-CENTERED

23–0 BC the enemy had total control. Rooted in my ideology, me! Before Christ, the devil had really taken hold. I lived a completely self-centered life. Arrogant and puffed up, climbing the ladder of fortune and fame. Exalting myself, creating a crown for an earthly domain. Trying to gain the whole world, claiming all that there is to claim. That was my story, guts chasing after the glory. Others have another story. Some just want to fit in, be a part of the gang. Always seeming to stand out, never measuring up to what they feel is enough. Not cool enough, smart enough, attractive or athletic enough. Ego/self-esteem, high or low, still centered in self. Some have a great career, nice income. Building plans for a family. Girlfriend soon to be fiancé, then you marry. You're all in, in this world of sin, so much so that you don't even count your soul among the valuable. Focused only on the here and now. Never realizing you were created for so much more! Back to me and this self-centered society. I was humbled beyond belief, brought low down to the ground! High was my goal, will was strong, still brought low. Looking everywhere, every door closed. Nowhere left to turn but within. That's where I found Him! The end of BC life for me, when The Lord knocked at the door of my heart. He had been there but had to close all other doors for me to realize I had been chosen by Him! Ground zero/1 AD my eyes were truly opened to see that the Lord was with me all the time. He created me for something divine. He orchestrated it all to bring me here in Him! Anno Domini (AD); The year of our Lord! The year it stopped being about me! The year I begin, born again in Him as He enters and uses my body for His Glory! His mouthpiece, His conduit, His vessel, His tabernacle, His hands and feet on the earth! I'm given visions, I dream dreams in Destiny, destined to become a reality! 23 AD I'm not what I should be, but I'm still serving the Lord and haven't gotten tired yet. However, my flesh gets up off the table of sacrifice quite often. Turning back to self-centered thinking. Spirit so willing, but flesh so weak! If my mind could just keep stayed on you. So many distractions make it impossible. In all things, You are the center! So why do I keep edging you out with stuff? Next thing I know, I'm back centered in self. Tearing down my own health with bad habits, when I'm supposed to be your tabernacle, blameless and holy. Bad habits turn to addictions and the enemy puts me back in shackles with thefts, lies and robberies! Lost my focus, cost me my freedom. This place is becoming a dwelling place for demons! Clean me up, from the inside out! Give me another chance to walk upright and be right with you!

—Scripture References—
Philippians 1:21, Luke 11:24–26, Matthew 23:12, Revelation 3:20

THE RACE

A race is run; a pace has begun. When I began running my race, I didn't know the duration. So, running at a furious pace, I took off. Faster and faster, I went. So fast I felt my feet leaving the ground. Looking around, no one was in front of me. Could it be this easy? The path started off smooth, but then got ruff with stuff, obstruction after obstruction. Going so fast, if I fell now, it could have been my destruction. Still, not slowing down with so much momentum behind me. Feet barely touching the ground. Moving so fast that it blinded me. I had enthusiasm, excitement, and fervor right beside me. Still, no one was in front of me. I was flying high and thought I would never come down. But from behind me, I could feel something; I heard a sound. On my back a sensation, a push. What a rush! This acceleration has got to be a plus. But what I didn't see was the cliff ahead of me. Tumble, tumble, thump, crack, pop! Not going to hop up from this. Now I'm down in the valley, feeling my own mortality with shadows lurking all around me. Pain and fear grip me, but then I hear, "Low, I am with thee." I was ministered to, laid down for a few, then realized what I had to do. Rise and get back in the race. But in reflection, what was that push, that voice? The enemy was distracting me, and he knew he couldn't stop me by standing in my way. So, he got behind me and blind-sided me. But hold on, I was already blinded. Blinded because I had always been focused on me! Time to change the strategy, change up the pace. This is not a sprint, or a tough man competition. Endurance is needed from beginning to the end. Still need to run like I'm trying to win. So here I am, still running. But no longer am I running for me. Now I'm running for You!

—Scripture References—
1 Corinthians 9:24, Ecclesiastes 9:11, Galatians 5:7, 2 Timothy 4:7, Acts 20:24, Matthew 24:13

MY EYES

Aiesha Pyles thought she had it all figured out. Get ahead, schemes and smiles met with growing clout. The world was her oyster. In a dog-eat-dog world, she was going to get her pearl! Never entered her mind, at the time, that she ever did anything wrong at all. Hustle hard, grind and shine while looking good all at the same time! What else, in the world, could life be worth living for?

Jason Ross dedicated his entire career to philanthropic endeavors. Though he was a boss, he never flossed, just sought to build up heavenly treasures, beyond measure! This man had it all figured out. Charity, family first with God's Word his guiding light, above all. Hustle hard, grind and shine while looking good all at the same time! What else, in the world, could life be worth living for?

Melissa Trist was a mother first, laying her career aside. Dedicating her life to God and boy, that's when times became hard! A controlling husband felt he was losing control, which injured his pride. He was used to bringing her everything and was not prepared to share. Long struggle, short story, she got thrown out of her house, lost her kids, left to fend for herself in the streets. Rejected in her search for job after job. Cunning, savvy people with more work experience would always win out. Finally got a job but lost it when someone used their pull to push her out. Back on the street with no food to eat. Nothing left but faith. She thought, *Lord, if You could just help me get back on my feet, I could get a place, get a lawyer, get my kids back and get to see the look on that controlling man's face when all the bad he has done has been erased!*

Aiesha Pyles came into that fateful day when she met face-to-face with God. No longer able to get over on schemes and smiles, God said, "Look into My eyes!" She could finally see through her Creator's Eyes, what He intended for her to be. An object used as an example of His GRACE, His MERCY, for His GLORY! Instead, she chose the low road, the broad road ending in destruction! She was able to see, through God's eye, that she never had love. Only interested in selfish gain. She got her pearl but lost her soul. She saw all the people she hurt and how. The name, Melissa Trist, came up. Long forgotten, but now remembered. Aiesha never was even interested in her position. Just didn't like the way she looked and was so used to taking, she took her livelihood away! "So, continue to walk, but your road has come to an end! An object of WRATH and RIGHTEOUS INDIGNATION you were created for!"

Jason Ross came into that fateful day when he met face-to-face with God. Jason was expecting a warm and well received greeting, but God just looked at him sternly and said, "Look into My eyes!" He was finally able to see how God created him to be in relationship with. Though Jason knew and followed the Word, he didn't have love, he only sought out the benefits without a sincere and loving heart. He sought to control everything in his life, and since he knew he could not control God, he never had a true relationship with Him. So all of His good deeds were burned up, as they didn't prove true through the fire. What's more, though he put family first, his controlling ways made him treat the closest people in his life the worst! He saw all the people he hurt. The name, Melissa Trist, came up. Was Melissa Ross before their divorce. "You had so much, but you never had love and now you're left with nothing!"

Melissa Trist came into that fateful day when she met face-to-face with God. "Well done, you upright and faithful servant! You have finished your race and had a great pace that put you in first place!" There was a judgment seat prepared for her. God said, "You have been chosen to judge the earth. Look into My eyes and all will be revealed!" Mansions in heaven, eternal love more abundant than anyone could ever dream of! Connected to the vine for once and for all time! What else, in the world, could life be worth living for?

—Scripture References—
Matthew 7:21–23, Luke 9:25, 2 Timothy 4:7, Philippians 2:14–16, Hebrews 12:1,
1 Corinthians 9:24

PRECIPICE

We all share a common pain. We all have a promise. Take away everything, this one thing remains. God is for us! Hated and manipulated for who we are. At least it used to be plain, in the open. Now, secretly, they plot their agenda while smiling and even putting on our face. Infiltrating and converting, defiling and perverting from within. Immersed in a world of sin, our clothes have become blood stained, because we're one with them. Trapped in a web, worldwide. The prince of the air roams and stares, looking to chew you up and swallow. The pinnacle of this diabolical plan for theft, death and destruction of man will become our precipice! This is also the time where rhyme meets reason, and we enter the season of preparation. The evil in righteous men had to be driven far from them, through trials and great tribulation. Only then will the church begin to truly honor The Lord. True community, true love, a real family. It took this precipice to finally become one! Known by our Love, one faith, one baptism, one God above all! Here we stand, at the precipice, Christian!

—Scripture References—
Ephesians 2:1–10, John 10:10, Matthew 10:22, 1 Peter 5:8

LITTLE THINGS

Work in the morning, setting my alarm, slipped my mind. Somehow something woke me right on time. Supposed to be cold and cloudy. Somehow something told me don't overdress. The whole day it was warm and sunny. Another day, somehow something made me want to wear my waterproof hoody, even though there was no forecast of rain. Sure enough, the sky blasts open with a thunderous roar, so loud I almost hit the floor! Something I thought, money is safe in a bank. Somehow something told me, take your money out. Banks closed for the day, criminal activities in my account. Couldn't take from me any amount. Just one day of mercies, too many to count. So great is our God. Still, I see Him in all the little things.

—Scripture References—
Matthew 10:30

FINISH LINE

The drummer beats his drum, signaling what is to come. The battle has just begun, as the soldiers ready their weapons. But the war has already been won, even before the battlefield was ever even stepped on! This is the victory that God has given His people. This world, we will all overcome! It may not seem that's the way it will be, but one day you will see, greater is He that is in We than he that is in the world. That is our victory! Don't need to be fast or strong, just endure to the end. Keep going like we're trying to win until we get to our finish line. If you ride inside a train, and you go into a tunnel, everything gets dark. You still maintain your cool. No panic ripped up tickets ready to jump out. The train still reaches its destination right on time. So why are you ready to quit before you reach your finish line? The light shines in the darkness and the darkness will not overcome it. The victory that we have, not knowing the end outcome, we already know we've overcome, by faith. We see with our spiritual eyes, not our hands, the plans God has for us. Though the day is dark, all I need to do is endure to see a new day knowing that's not the way He said it would end for me. We will arrive at our destination right on time. We will achieve our destiny! We will have our victory! We will make it to the finish line!

—Scripture References—
1 John 5:4, Mark 13:13, 1 Samuel 17:47, Revelation 12:11

93

STUCK

Incognito, I go into position, stuck on fickle people's feelings. If they only knew that I was listening. Hearing what they think about me, what they speak when I'm not around. I thought they believed in me, but as soon as they think I'm not there, the truth becomes clear. Forgot all I'd learned, focused solely on the here and now. Stuck in the quicksand. Faith dissipated, direction changed, consumed in doubt! Why didn't it work out the way it was supposed to? Why do I still find myself here?

—Scripture References—
Matthew 5:11 and 12

SOLDIERS

Soldiers in the army of the Lord. Redeemed by His Word, by the blood of the Lamb and our testimony. Bound to Christ in holy matrimony. A peculiar people. Slayed daily, swayed nearly. Still putting all our trust in the One who enlisted us. Warriors of love, even toward our enemy. Haters of this present world. I once was blind, but now I see with my spiritual eye. Physical sight blinds me from my spirituality. That's why I close my eyes when I pray. Promised all eternity but still taking it day by day. Confident and bold, yet humble to a fault. Pain and death portrayed as a work of art. I must confess, our math does test, being that less is more and more is less. When you're poor and persecuted, you're blessed. Wisdom in God is foolishness to the world. Peculiar indeed how blood red, when He bled, made us snow white. A hundred men can put ten thousand to flight. Still discernment does protest these truths we hold to be self-evident amongst God's people, prevalent. Inevitably, these truths will be known to all. These peculiar people will be revealed to all creation. Then all nations will see, peculiar is what they all wish they could be.

—Scripture References—
2 Timothy 2:3 and 4, Luke 9:23, 2 Corinthians 4:7–12, Job 13:15, Revelation 12:11, Leviticus 26:8

95

TRUTH, WAY, LIFE

So little time, so much to do. True! Some spend a lifetime chasing the wind. What's important in life, some do not have a clue. Embracing lies from the beginning, false facts, wrong ideologies. Lost in a web of deception. If only they could find the truth!

Fire burning, light bright with darkness all around. Strange sounds behind, making you want to rush ahead, but even with the light, the path is not clear. More than one path, but which is the way to make it home. The wide path looks appealing, as it seems to be well traveled, yet the road less traveled, though narrow, is the way.

Love gives, life takes life for the sake of extending its own. Love gave its own life for the sake of all the souls of the world! With our soul focus on pleasing us. Preparing for Him, He's preparing a place for us. He is the groom, we are the wife. Jesus The Truth, The Way and The Life!

—Scripture References—
John 14:6

STDs

Bless me please, I'm screaming while I'm bringing about my own sabotage! Why don't things ever work for me, everything always seems to be working against me? The real question is, why do you compromise your spirituality in physicality turning into illegality, bringing about curses on your own body? Carrying the form of godliness, the norm for a society oppressed, denying the true power of God. The key can be found in the reality of the times. This life is not the prize! Realize with spiritual eyes that your body is God's property! How can you believe a physical remedy can be found in a problem rooted in life? Spiritually transmitted demons, the STD's they don't talk about! Familiar sin, familiar spirits enter in when you do the dirty, sexual immorality. Thinking you're outsmarting God with protective contraceptives. Condoms can't protect you from these STD's. Sinning against your own body. Lining up agents designed to bring about your own demise. Stealing all God has for you, robbing vitality from your body. If they don't kill you prematurely, they'll orchestrate things to destroy your destiny! Though condoms may lock in your semen, demons cannot be contained by rubbers. Unleashing self-destruction on God's plan for your life, if it's not your wife. What will be your stance for your seed outside of marriage? Abstinence is the only true protection, cold showers for an erection. Sex outside of marriage, the dysfunction God is facing. Running with the masses in a world of sin, what are you chasing? Most people only see in hindsight the problems they created for themselves, trying to find a way away from serving God. Power in purpose seems so hard when not following The Master's plan. Patience is a virtue, if you could just wait for all things to be revealed you would see what always has been known. All power's in His Hands!

—Scripture References—
1 Corinthians 6:18, 2 Thessalonians 2:9, Matthew 28:18–20

NEW DAY

A new day, new mercies! Not gonna look back no more! Yesterday, I was hungry and thirsty, but somehow, the Lord, He did fill me. Had no money, no place to sleep, but somehow, the Lord, He sheltered me. Was feeling awfully dirty, and just then, a rain came in. Cleansed me and my clothes. Gust of wind and the sun dried me from head to toe. Just when I begin to get weary in my soul and tired in my body, I lay down to rest wherever the Lord leads me. Then, I wake up to a new day, new mercies! Not gonna look back no more!

—Scripture References—
Lamentations 3:23, James 2:5, Matthew 6:25–34

FALLEN

Dear Lord, how far have we fallen in this land? How bloody and dirty have become these hands? How far have we strayed from You? It's getting harder to hear You. Sometimes I don't even feel You. In a state of panic, I draw out this appeal to You! Do You even hear me, or am I drowned out in all this iniquity? A crazy land, this has become. Every generation worse than the last one. A Godless generation we're in, still believing the society operates in propriety. How far have we fallen in this land, offering You tokens of appreciation without the power of love identifiable at all. Not knowing, not having Your Word on their lips. No time to study and meditate upon Your word, but when trouble arises the first name cried out, "God!" or, "Jesus!" No surprise they go back to the source of protection and comfort when in a panic. Still denying Him daily as they frantically store up earthly treasures. An entire society solely lost! The pain of seeing a world in a whirlwind turning in vain, going down the drain. Have we fallen so far that we cannot return to You? Your people still trust in You, not storing where treasures will rust. Your people eagerly wait for You to return to us!

—Scripture References—
2 Timothy 3:1–5

STORED UP WRATH

Drops of blood wet the earth. Blood, sweat, and tears all shed at the same time! Unbearable pain, excruciatingly insane! How can a man do this to another man? Gain pleasure from another's pain? Oh, son of man, how much evil you do! You know not what you do to the son of man, the Son of God. Entertaining for them to see, my Jesus bleed. They gave Him vinegar to drink, laughing and mocking as He was dying. To think all the dark powers and principalities focused on this very hour. The ninth hour is here, here on Calvary! Dark indeed, with dark clouds looming. Luminous the day that tore Jesus' vessel away! So, after the body was spent, the veil in the temple was also rent. The veil unveiled; all power revealed in the hand of Him that rose again! If only He would have stayed but had to go away and prepare a place so we would be together properly in glory. If they only knew the righteous indignation stored up for them that would deny Him. The dark powers, so foolish to do this, thinking they would extinguish, only to ignite and unleash the Beast, the Lion of Judah! Wrath and judgment on judgment day for those that refuse to follow the way. What a rebellious generation today! Stubbornness and rebellion as the sin of witchcraft. Fire burning, lion roaring, plagues, and tormenting! Vengeance is the Lord's and even them that crucified Jesus shall see. Dark was that day, and so shall this day be. But after the darkest night, comes the dawn. Violence did reside so that peace can abide. Millennial reign of peace on earth with Jesus again! No longer the son a man, but He still calls me friend.

—Scripture References—
Proverbs 18:24; Matthew 27:32–54; Revelation 5:5, 19:11–21, 20:1–10; 1 Thessalonians 5:2; Amos 5:18–20

HE DID IT

Miraculous metamorphosis made! A change overcame him, her and me. Never the same again. Touch by Heaven. He did it! I've seen Him do it! Doctors determine the end; disease is going to win. Might as well get your house in order. Dead man walking! God turned that report around, turn that frown upside down. Life will continue, it will not quit! He did it! I've seen Him do it! Funds, insufficient, money funny, should have dried up a long time ago. Gifts and inheritances, canceled debts and surprise checks in the mail kept me afloat when I would have drowned in poverty. God did it! I've seen Him do it! His merciful kindness is great toward us. Miraculous miracles He does perform. No one wants to be sick or poor, but in your weakness, He shows himself strong. Love projected, power perfected, miracles proliferated! In the end, the greatest truth manifested. He just wants to show you that you need Him. So easy to forget in a world full of industry and technology. The roaring of the world drown out His sweet soft words in your inner ear. Sometimes, when He finally gets your attention, you have run out of time. Life is at an end. Since He now knows your weakness has made you focus solely on Him, miracles make a way for you to continue living! A second chance at life, another chance to get it right. God did it and it is miraculous in our sight!

—Scripture References—
2 Corinthians 5:17 and 12:9, Galatians 6:15, John 12:37–41, Mark 12:11

TODAY

This is the day called - today! Now is the only creation in play. Such a blessing to be in the land of the living while it's still called today. Yesterday gone, full of memories locked in time. All you've gone through has prepared you for now! A miraculous mystery, how through all antiquity of history and time, so many dead and gone, but you stand here in the newness of life! Never has there been a day just like today, nor will there ever be again. Such a privilege to be a part of something God has given you to enter into. Conversations, interactions, transactions, not merely materially but spiritually manifested. Much more going on than your five senses ever detected. In the "now" of time you find all material life. Opportunities, possibilities for good works producing good fruit to be stored up for all eternity. Rest needed, but time wasted is such a travesty. You're in the now of time to leave a legacy for all time! Gifts and treasures lie dormant inside you, meant to be circulating in the mix, now! Percolating within, urging to get out. Urgency sensed! Act while it's still called today! Time is of the essence. The essence of life is here and now! Bring your presence and focus to bear on all the immediate. Cares and distractions lay aside. Don't take lightly the priority of action. What if you knew tomorrow you would die? What would your today look like? What if your eternity was a constant image of all your missed opportunities? Wouldn't that be hell? Now is the time to let your light shine up on the hill! Complacent in comfort, come out! Paralyzed in fear, come out! Centered in self, come out! Sunken in negativity, come out! Pilfering in pettiness, come out! Drowning in depression, come out! Festering in unforgiveness, come out! In the name of Jesus, come out from all that hinder you and do all God created you for! A time for rest and a time for play. A time for everything, under the Sun. When it's time for good works, never take for granted, TODAY!

—Scripture References—
Hebrews 3:13

WAITING ON THE LORD

Good things come to those who wait. Thank the Lord, every day, no matter what He puts on your plate. Eat it all and be glad. Courage to face all wins the day. Though hard it may be, still necessary. Even Jesus asked for His cup to pass, as he sweat drops of blood in the garden. But before his last breath, one testimony left. It is finished! For His obedience, His love, and sacrifice gained power over all with a name above all. Good things come to those who wait. Even Paul asked for the thorn in his side to be removed. The demon sent to buffet and get him out of his groove. Still, God didn't move. He stayed the course, kept the faith, finished his race, and got to see the look on God's face. Well pleased, all sins erased. Good things come to those who wait. Discipline is gratification differed. A sin sick generation, impulsive and obsessive, compulsive and possessive. Needing, wanting, undisciplined, flaunting. No patience, no time, except to grind and gain whatever's on their mind. But good things come to those who wait. If you get it all now, what will be your fate? If you give your all now, training your mind and body, bridling your tongue, subduing your flesh, you will pass your test. Needless to stress or debate. Great things come to those who wait on the Lord! Strength renewed, flying high above the valley. Looking down just to see how far you've come. Treasures stored up, forever to be enjoyed. Joy unspeakable, peace unthinkable, love eternal. All creation restored. Divine nature and harmony. I get to be with Jesus, and all things adored. All because I patiently waited on the Lord!

—Scripture References—
Psalm 27:14, 33:20, 37:9 and 34, 123:2, 130:5 and 6; Isaiah 40:31; Luke 12:36

THE SPIRIT OF THE LORD

When the Spirit of the Lord is poured out on His people, we corporately become one body. Glory raised in praise. Glory comes in waves. Hearing the worship of the congregation, highs and lows flows succinctly. When the Spirit of the Lord rests upon my heart, I feel a joy so full, unspeakable! I know I'm a part of the great celebration, for here I am, celebrating! I am dancing and singing, clapping and rejoicing, praising as a part of the victory confirmation. When the Spirit of the Lord comes upon my spirit, my spirit soars! Out of my body, closer to the Lord. Not thinking about what happens after, or what happened before. This moment, all that is! When my body calms down, calls my spirit back down, the Spirit of the Lord is still there with me, ministering to and comforting me. When my body breaks down, my spirit returns to God, my soul will rest in peace. When the Spirit of the Lord comes upon my soul, death and the grave will be deleted, the devil defeated, and I rise to the newness of life! Way back when the Spirit of the Lord first entered me, that was when I received my guarantee that I would forever be with the Lord! He sealed me, when the Spirit of the Lord came upon me and confirmed with my spirit. No longer needing to worry, you are God's property!

—Scripture References—
2 Corinthians 3:17 and 18

LITTLE THING

Every little thing I can do for You, I will do. I'm just a little thing, and little things I do. Put together all the little things in my little life, still a small thing. Walking all day, still got nowhere. Running all night just to make it up there. Coming down now, for heights I do fear. If You're with me, though, I can go anywhere!

—Scripture References—
Hebrews 2:6–11, Philippians 4:13

HUES

Hues of blue cascade across my heart. The blues are the days, absorbing every shade 'til nothing is left but gray. Resentment from outward conditions turns inward to depression. Everything is rubbing me the wrong way! Coarse and rough becomes this heart. Flesh and bone, turning into stone. I forgot to guard my heart. Slipped my mind, I'm still behind enemy lines. War is hard! It's not supposed to be easy. The more a threat, the more attacks from the enemy. Isolated and alone, targeted and attacked! Don't know how much more I can take! Flat on my back, from blow after blow! Hues of gray cascade across my face. Every shade gets darker 'til all that's left is total darkness. What a dark day! Darkness conceals the truth, producing grief and gnashing of teeth. Proliferating lies behind discouragement, pain, and fear. You should just quit. Go on and end it. Kill yourself! Nobody would miss you anyway. But I rebuke the enemy in the name of Jesus! I will live and not die! I will proclaim the goodness of the Lord in the land of the living! I will serve; I will endure! I will keep the faith! I will finish this race! Hues of bright lights cascade across my soul. Every tone enraptured my essence. Finally made it home, back into His presence!

—Scripture References—
John 22:29; 2 Corinthians 7:6; Lamentations 3:20; Psalm 27:4, 42:5, 116:10, 118:17; Ezekiel 18:28, 36:26; 2 Timothy 4:7; Proverbs 4:23; Ephesians 6:12

CORPORATE WORSHIP

A place where souls dwell. Mind body and soul intertwine. Access the primordial mind, with spiritual effervescence at the essence. Mind stimulation as you swim in the saturation that is Him. Soul confirmation as you begin to pray that this never ends. Blended lives, star crossed lovers. Mending ties, as we tend to each other's wounds. Building up, never breaking down these blessings we have found. Much more profound than the building blocks of love's desire, the final product of love's empire.

—Scripture References—
1 Peter 2:9

WILDERNESS

Stuck deep in this wilderness. I can't see the forest for the trees. Technology has gone out on me. Lost my rifle when I fell down that hill. Back to square zero, depressed I confess, standing deep in the wilderness. I hear howls, growls and roars. Ravenous animals on the prowl and I'm stuck out here alone and defenseless. Trying to make sense of how I got here, seems senseless. Like being stuck behind enemy lines, in the trenches. Scared to come out with the enemy all about. Still, greater is He who lives in me. Realizing I'm not alone, courage returns, and I leave my hiding place. I must subdue the land and find my way. Crooked paths made straight as we prepare the way for The Lord!

—Scripture References—
Revelation 12:6, Matthew 4:1, Isaiah 40:3

M-O-N-E-Y

All eyes glare into the frame. Focused on this one thing. To my surprise, vain was the gaze. Amazed at the fact that tokens, money was meant to mean everything. Lovers of money, users of others. Isn't money supposed to be used and people loved? Confused to see the sad truth of our society. The root of all evil, switching priorities. In essence, better to give than receive. Totally deceived, profiting in selfish ambition. Gaining all the world's treasures. After your last breath, what do you have left? You surely can't take it with you. Not only have you lost everything, but you also lost the thing that is your very being! You lost your soul, chasing after fool's gold. This shallow theme, perpetuated through media and entertainment, bombards us, taking our focus away from where it really needs to be. Albeit money is a necessity until it is not. Springing up out of the root of all types of evil, appears the mark of the beast! The trap has been set, dangling the bait in front of your face. Chasing fast-changing currency that will soon no longer be. Once lured into the trap, the only thing left from your love of money will be slavery! Marked as the property of the enemy!

—Scripture References—
1 John 2:15 and 16, 4:4 and 5, 5:4 and 5; James 1:12, 4:4; John 15:19; 2 Peter 2:4–10; Colossians 2:20; 2 Corinthians 7:31; 2 Kings 6:16 and 17; 2 Timothy 3:1 and 2; Luke 16:13; 1 Timothy 6:10; Matthew 16:26; 1 Peter 5:4; Revelation 13:16, 14:9; Ecclesiastes 10:19

SLEEPING WITH THE ENEMY

Cold sweats, sleepless nights. Unsettled in my soul. Past regrets treacherously consume me as I lay, sleeping with the enemy. Dreaming carries me away but never truly leaves. Have become one, stuck with the enemy! As I rise, the enemy is right there with me. To my surprise, in the mirror, his reflection I see. Evil incarnate, staring right back at me! My carnal nature, this flesh, the evil I speak about. Can't run nor hide, and no getting out! Poisoning and perverting my mind. Self-seeking, with demand, starving out my spirit man. Holy Spirit, help me to subdue this flesh! Flesh is weak, and I am willing but weaker at best. Only by your Spirit can I pass this test. So even though I am weary in my soul, as though I had any other choice, I'll keep sleeping with the enemy, with losses and victory, until my strength is renewed. Waiting for that great day when I finally and completely put down corruptibility!

—Scripture References—
Galatians 5:17, Romans 7:14–20, Mark 14:38, Isaiah 40:31

THE VISION

Right down the vision and make it plain. Growing pains may remain until the end. The enemy gains by stealing. Destiny will not be denied, even though it may not be what you thought. Though experiencing the death of your vision, resurrection is in His hands. Your heart's desires play a part but not the whole. The plan, you'll only see a glimpse of. Control remains with Him that knows all. You play a small part of a very big picture, so don't think of yourself higher than you should. So great the landscape as God paints His masterpiece! His hand and plan upon every man from the greatest to the least. He has given you the ability to dream dreams, which in destiny become a reality! Never give up on godly dreams. Though they may tarry, wait for it! Oh, so vivid, so real! Repeating with regularity, adding clarity. After the vision's been written and before provisions are given, remember this because it is of the utmost importance. Proper preparation prevents poor performance!

—Scripture References—
John 10:10; 2 Corinthians 1:12, 11:15; Ezekiel 11:24; Daniel 10:7; Acts 18:1; Romans 12:3

MESSENGER

God intends to send a message far, far away, needs someone trustworthy. The lost but not forgotten need a lifeline right on time! The message needs to be sent in a timely manner. Who will be my messenger? Moving so fast you get blasted in a sting, caught along the path of the blur. Angel wings, bringing glory to the King of kings. Send him, my mighty messenger! Service due, servants true. Serving the almighty, nothing's impossible! Harbinger of death to the creatures of wrath meant for destruction, given to the seductions of the world. Protection for the chosen, sealed for the day of redemption. Circling hovering never left alone! There to bow down at the very throne of The Father and the Lamb. Messenger, the very extension of the Godhead! Failed to mention, also our brethren. Angels in heaven and angels on earth. One third fallen, found on scorched earth. Man, too fallen, formed from the earth. Angels calling', many men too. Still few chosen, so what are you here to do? A messenger on assignment or fallen bound in chains. What message do you contain?

—Scripture References—
Isaiah 40:9, Revelation 19:10 and 22:10, 2 Chronicles 16:9

I AM

I am a product of my environment. I am a genetic curse. I am made responsible for atrocities of many incidents many generations before me, forced to carry out the same. I am the condition within my family. I am a consequence of sin, shaped in iniquity. I am degeneration, I am degradation. Many nations forced to face the same trace of similitude. Many lost in sin, faced with the shadows that cover them. Darkness consumes identity, forcing me to identify with that which is lost, cut off! My identity can't be with that which covers me! I am not the evil in me! I am not that grievous sin! I am not the sum of my actions while evil is allowed to enter in. I am in agreement with the word wholeheartedly. Still, there remains something unholy in my body! Before I knew what sin was, it was there. Tearing at my soul to devour and drag me down beneath the ground in condemnation! Still, the great I AM always had in mind a different destination. What remains is what was there from the very beginning. All that pertains to my true identity. I am a child of the most high God! I am an overcomer! I am more than a conqueror through the blood of Jesus! I am the head and not the tale. I am a lender not a borrower. Though evil may be allowed to lend a portion of my being right now, that's not what I am. Every portion lent shall be returned! Purged through the fire, burned to nothing, everything that condemns. Still, I stand. When the time arrives and there are no more corruptible parts in me, it will finally be revealed what I am!

—Scripture References—
1 John 3:2 and 5:4, 1 Corinthians 15:57, James 1:13–15, 1 Peter 4:12–19

MOURNING

A sullen gaze. Seeming to be looking in your direction but staring straight through you. I don't even see you. The only thing I see are memories of days when she was here. Reminiscing when we would caress and love and play. My confidant, my best friend, unexpectedly passed away! Take not for granted today, tomorrow promised to nobody. Appreciate every good gift given in this life. Cherish each moment knowing, eventually, that gift will be taken away. A sullen gaze still has me in a daze, but all praise be to the Lord God Almighty for giving me the gift of life, for Grace and making the ultimate sacrifice! Thank you, Lord, for ensuring my beloved a place in heaven, that I may see her again! Still, at a time of mourning, my sullen gaze remains. Would pay any cost to remove the pain, void, grief from my heart, as I mourn her loss.

—Scripture References—
Ecclesiastes 3:4

CONTENT

Money came, money went. So fast it goes so fast it's spent. Try to hold on to a couple dollars, but the bills will not relent! Had a career, but careless mistakes or strategic mishaps caused my career to go down the toilet. Used to be popular, but when I gave my life to Christ, I started being avoided. On a boat with one passenger and one life raft. A crack in the hull and she jumps ship, leaving me in descent. I've been all the way up and been all the way down. Have learned to, in all things, be content. Good and bad befalls us all, but of this one thing I'm confident. No matter where I may be, I'm God's property and I know He's got me!

—Scripture References—
Philippians 4:10–13

PERSECUTION

Blessed is he that endures persecution for right standing in Christ! If you deny Him before men, the same will be said of you when wanting to enter into heaven. Our brethren on the front lines surrounded by enemy eyes, face the pressure of compromise, just to live in peace. Freedom of religion is not to be taken for granted. So sheltered, in America, and need to be aware of our brothers in other parts of the planet. One day a woman came to me and said, "My testimony seems phony when I testify about the most high. I feel no pressure to hold me down with no persecution around. It's become a token saying with no meaning, whether spoken out loud or praying. Bible gaining dust, frustrated in my walk and lust for life. Never satisfied, but satisfaction will not be denied. So, I acknowledge the Lord before men, but my will still bends to sin. Am I redeemed or condemned?" This same young woman became a missionary. Went abroad to share her token testimony. Came to a land that soon had their government overthrown. Had she known, she surely would've never become a missionary. Freedoms lost in a communist regime. Seems impossible to make it back home. She began thinking about that bible gaining dust in the den. Reminded when there was no pressure or persecution. The reason she began thinking about that bible is because this newly occupying government had the audacity to outlaw Christianity! No bibles permitted in any sanctuary! Now, as a missionary she finds her faith truly put to the test. No more token gestures, acknowledging Christ before men could mean death! As fear subsides, peace enters in. The power of love becomes evident. This is what you were created for! There is no need to fear man when I'm a part of God's plan! So, I strap on my sandals for the journey. Missionary, my mission is mission impossible with an entire government against me, but greater us He.... Y'all don't hear me! I've found my mission; I have a true testimony. No more tokens in mundane routines and complacency. No more do I take for granted the

116

Word of The Almighty! Taken out of comfort, stripped of what I've taken for granted. Ignited in the flames of passion and purpose, in the same Spirit that seals me as God's property! Blessed is he that willingly drinks from the cup of persecution for the sake of righteousness, for the same will be engrafted into God's family. Now, that finally has meaning to me!

—Scripture References—
2 Timothy 2:3, Matthew 10:28, 32 and 33, 1 John 4:4

STRANGE THING

Can't sleep at night. Awaken in torment. Must be the witching hour! Tossing, convulsing, shaking and turning! Spiritual wickedness is at work along with dark powers. Trying to seize my body while I rest. Cold sweats and then feel like I'm burning. Is this a punishment for sin or yet another test? Or simply the enemy trying to devour me? Such a dark night, I think I'll turn on a light and praise His Holy Name 'til dawn! Dark powers withdrawn. A new day awakens like nothing ever happened at all. Nothing left to say, no one would probably believe me anyway. So, I just shake it off and thank God for a brand-new day with new mercies. Not thinking it to be strange, the fiery trials that come to test me. Knowing the enemy doesn't waste ammunition, that's just more confirmation that I'm in God's family!

—Scripture References—
Ephesians 6:12, James 1:2–4, 1 Peter 4:12 and 13

YOUR GLORY

Use me for Your Glory, giving me divinity in Thee. Lifting holy hands for Your Glory, though my sticky fingers have robbed even You. Doing a dance for Your Glory, though I've danced with devils too. Living a sacrificial life for Your Glory, but the problem with a living sacrifice is that it keeps getting up off the altar. Created for Your Glory but, in selfishness, did falter. For Your Glory, I would do anything! So many things I wish I could undo. Revelation truth revealed to me, in Glory, an epiphany. I clap my hands, do a dance, sing praises unto Thee—not solely for Your Glory, but also because You deposited in me a celebration for the victory, my inheritance in Glory! You worked it all out, work it together for my good and for Your Glory!

—Scripture References—
Romans 8:15–17; Psalm 16:11, 57:11, 86:9–12, 134:2; 1 Timothy 2–8; Revelation 4:11

CURSE

To You is praise. Praise like a hummingbird flapping its wings. Praise like the mockingbird when it sings. Praise like new life in spring. To You is Glory. Glory like the rising Sun. Glory like a battle won. Glory like a curse undone. But what about me? I am under a curse! Please take this curse away! Salty sweat blinds my eyes but cleanses my body of toxins ingested when I devoured some animal's body parts. My daughter crying, because that was one of her farm friends. In preparing that thing, had to clean him out and found some devoured body parts in him. Her tears soothe her soul but arouse my guilt. Cleansing water wash away the salt and toxins from the surface of my body from the sweat of the day. All this cleansing makes me feel better, but I'm still dirty! Can't wash the blood off my hands. Can't get this dirt from under my fingernails. I am under a curse! Please take this curse away from me! I vow to, in all things, give You praise but days like this makes the world seem so cold! In a land where you have to take life to perpetuate your own. I found an injured animal. His flesh not appealing to me, so I befriended him. Cleaned his wounds and set him out in the Sun. By the time I return, he's covered in ants trying to devour him alive. I guess his flesh was pleasing to them. This is a cursed land! Politicians always lying, but I'm still supposed to vote, for who? All have been compromised by lies. It's like a requirement of the position, like lawyers saying anything to win their case. This whole world is cursed! The test - amid this perplexity of curses, can you still give praise and glory to God? Praise like the birds when they sing. Praise like new life in spring. Glory with each rising of the Sun. If you can then that's another battle won, that's another curse undone!

—Scripture References—
Genesis 50:20

WORK

I have a daily mind state that failure is not an option, though failure seems to be my occupation. When standing up to the light of the best of the best, I must confess being put to the test has me looking a mess! Still, on my plate I feel a heavy burden. Should I wait until I have my own self straight or walk in my anointing? I have been constrained by this great gospel, forever to worship you! That means I must serve you too. Can't wait 'til I'm perfect to do what you called me to do, or I'll be waiting 'til I'm sitting in Glory with questions, why I didn't glorify You. Must work every day while it's still called today and know in my weaknesses and infirmities God will still make a way to get out of me what He deposited into me to tell this story, to His Glory!

—Scripture References—
Ephesians 5:20, Philippians 3:7–14, Hebrews 3:12–15

WAR

Men in pen suits writing with a designer pen a declaration of war. They've never been in war, never seen it up close, but decision makers send our children into battle by the droves. The stench of death over the land where man is forced to face his fellow man to a show down to decide what benefits men in pen suits. To them war is a conquest, a game of chess. People just pieces positions played for strategies outlaid. Mostly ponds, expendable property in an army of flesh. Standing against machines of metal meant to rip to shreds flesh and bone. Chemical warfare decimates droves without thought of repercussions. Atomic warfare meant to decimate entire cities and even countries. Protecting your homeland, your property and family, honorable it seems against dreams of conquest just for the pursuit of more. More land, more property and natural resources for your common man, expenses paid, blood of attrition. When is war truly an acceptable entity? A better cause than even freedom or protection of self is when flesh and blood is placed on the shelf. Spiritual warfare, laying aside carnal greed and pride. Fighting the good fight for all time's sake. Though your flesh they may still tear asunder, your soul they can't take, because you're fighting for the Creator. The most sinister plot in war is to gain power and control to steal all the Glory from the Lord. Such is the plot of Satan, that devil of old that deceives the whole world. To put it eloquently, the enemy subtly and gently replaces righteousness with what seems right, even if only for a night. Rudimentary tasks he'll give you a pass, just pick up man-made inventions for the sake of convenience. Wrapped up in it all the more 'til you become a slave to it, wondering how you ever lived without. Never satisfied, always wanting more, let's go to war and take theirs too! A world at war, chaos and confusion, famine, disease and pestilence. What is the solution? One man stands in the image of the beast, declaring to restore peace and harmony to the world. Just give me a single seat of absolute power and bow at my feet. The enemy uses war to turn men into beasts, 'til they're caught in the belly of the beast. Slavery from the greatest to the least. All forced to accept the mark of the beast!

—Scripture References—
Ephesians 6:10–17, Revelation 13 (entire chapter)

READY FOR WAR

Partners in defense to quench all the fiery darts of the wicked. The chest plate of righteousness, bulletproof vest with faith as my shield. The Author and Finisher of my faith already knew every attack I would sustain. Nothing gets through as long as my armor remains. Having on the mind of Christ with the helmet of salvation. Embracing godly meditation. Pants held up, buckle strapped tight with the truth. Steel toe boots, shard with the preparation of the Gospel. Creating godly conversation. I keep my boots ready to wear and share the Gospel wherever my feet may go. Last but not least, yeah you know, the Word! My double-edged sword! Offensively, I demolish all hostility, cutting to pieces all the traps of the enemy! Releasing chains of bondage, setting the captives free! Studying hard to show yourself approved! Due diligence with much studying done. I have my war clothes on now! I'm ready for war! I know I will still be standing in the end! Recovering all the lost, redeemed of every sin!

—Scripture References—
Ephesians 6:11–20, 2 Timothy 2:15, 2 Corinthians 15:58, Proverbs 16:6, Luke 4:18

DEBT PAID

I can't afford to live! Been giving my all, but it's never enough. Might as well dig my own grave. I don't deserve to live. I offend all of creation. What was I even created for? Nothing left I have to give. Good for nothing but taking. I take life just to extend my own. What I have was given, but I took what I never should have. In the book it is written, condemned to death! I can't afford not to live! I was given this life for a reason. The life I have I'll use to find a better life. Sacrifice fleshy gain to attain an imperishable crown. Can't stand this world, anyway, filled with misery and strife. There has to be a better way, under the footstool of the almighty. How can I get back in His good graces? There was a man who showed what the true race is and how to keep up the paces. If I follow His lead I can indeed live! Still nothing I do or give is ever enough. Only His sacrifice paid the price. Sealed by His Spirit, signed in the Lamb's book of life, paid in full!

—Scripture References—
2 Corinthians 1:18–22, Romans 6:23, 1 Corinthians 15:50–54

GRADUALLY

Trapped, locked in! In a world that bends men's will, to make us feel how they want us to feel. Condition our minds to think the way they want us to think, do what they want us to do. The American dream has us in a slumber. Programmed like machines as the devil takes us under. Pushed gradually towards a cliff, so slow so gradual. The prince of subtle deceit has been thinking on his feet. Enslaving minds programmed to believe they're the wardens and guards, when they're really inmates and time is really hard! Totalitarian, the system being ushered in. Diabolical control of all the women and the men. Wars waged to destabilize societies. Political agendas with lies and false propaganda. Technology promises comfort and convenience while ushering in enslavement. Brainwashing has been done when the script has been flipped from running technology to now being run. Gradual progress towards that cliff. Got to be more to do than just enjoy the view. I keep thinking I'm going to wake up from this nightmare of knowing where we're headed, while ignorance is bliss with people just tuned out to the signs and tuned in to technology. This can't be reality; this can't be possibly happening! Yet it is possible, it's just gradual. We'd never let Your creation be replaced by things virtual. Lord, please make a way for Your people!

—Scripture References—
Romans 12:2, Genesis 3:1, Revelation 13:16

HEART AND SOUL

If the heart is empty, mind contemplation is meaningless. If the soul has no depth, the heart is left with nothing but shallow emotions and will, more meaningless still. But rooted deep in the almighty, if the soul has a destiny, the Holy Spirit is it's guarantee. Poured into the soul a design, purpose in proportion to anointing. Rivers of life flowing into you, flowing through. Appointing a destiny to accomplish every assignment in a world bent on selfishness. The true test is being the best me I can be with selflessness as the key. Heart and soul combined, intertwined with His Spirit, I've found something so much greater than me. I've become a part, in union with the Almighty! There is nothing greater, oneness with my Savior! Soul recognition, hearts a glow. Heart and soul, mind illumination so bright I sense a halo! A day in the life of a worshiper, no other passion compares. Heart and soul connect with the almighty to tap into the source so I can share what He gave me. I've got to reach for the best that's in me, nothing ordinary will do. All my love, all my strength, all my heart and soul! Pouring out everything that's true, 'til nothing is left but dust and rubble. Finally, the heart fails, the soul sails and the spirit soars! Behold, at the appointed time, Glorified, Devine and restored with The Lord!

—Scripture References—
2 Corinthians 1:22, 1 Peter 2:9, Mark 12:29–31, Revelation 21:5

BAD SIDE

Foolish pride, self-consumed, mistreating your fellow man. Lining yourself up with God's bad side. Rushing into sin, the rush is what you chase. A must to embrace all things carnal. Lover of the world, despiser of God, heart hard as stone. Envy and jealousy, coveting everything you see. To steal is in your will. To kill gives you a thrill. Unable to create, only interested in destruction. Devised a grand plan to stand against your own Creator. Persuasion is your ally, as the father of lies, you raise up an army by your side. Legions of demons stand with you, droves of people too, but victory you never knew. The only thing you were created for was an antagonist in the story of heaven and earth. Every good story needs a villain; a problem presented, a conflict, a climax. All leading to the grand ending! Your original position, never really intended for you. An enemy implanted to stir up trouble. You play your part but never would get what you want. Instead, you get placed properly on God's bad side! At the climax, when the father of lies stands against the Truth, what will he have left to do? Once your purpose has run out and your time is up, when the harvest is ripe, wrath and vengeance, righteous judgment, and hell shall unveil! When the story is complete, the final victory's been won. After all is said and done, I hope you don't find yourself on God's bad side!

—Scripture References—
1 Kings 14:9; Romans 9:21 and 22; Revelation 14, 17 (entire chapters)

THOUGHT

I thought I caught the wind in my grasp. It eluded me alas. I taught a generation in legality and morality. They now teach me in levels of perversity I never knew. I puff myself up in knowledge and wisdom, bluff my way up to a "know it all." Pride preceded, my fall deleted all I thought I knew. I think I ought not have thought. Now, leaning not on the ladder, the ladder I climbed to cause so great a fall, just acknowledging You all my day in all my ways, trusting You to lead me through!

—Scripture References—
Proverbs 3:1–6 and 16:18, 1 Corinthians 8:1–3

THE EVIL IN ME

Wanting to look away but stay stuck like cement on a dump truck. Looking at a pair of legs like a leg of lamb at dinnertime. Supervisor, speaking to me unfairly. Wanted to hold my peace but, instead, gave him a piece of my mind two times! Didn't want to do it. It was the evil in me. Came crashing down like a rolling sea! People on the side of the road, trying to get home like me. Their car broke down, and they're looking at me desperately. Homeless man, panhandling, caught my eye with a plea. "Can you help me?" They both made me feel sorry, but "It's getting to be, where you can't trust anybody!" I say as I keep driving away. I wanted to stop, wanted to help. It was the evil in the world; the evil in me came crashing down like a rolling sea. I am a vessel of the Most High! This is my testimony, but I still find evil in me! My spirit, my mind, agrees with the Word, wholly, but in my flesh, something unholy. Struggles like this make me want to rip myself apart, then put the pieces back together again. How can I win when sin is having its way with me? The very enemy that I fight against! So intense, this struggle within my members. Will I ever find a solution? If you can manage these things, not a small thing but great things will be added to you. With His Spirit as your guide, the Lord on your side, all things are possible. So why does it seem that this evil in you has taken control altogether? Tongue out of control. Lungs filled with contempt. Every breath, an opportunity to vent! Not enough time spent devoted to the weapons of your warfare. Not enough time spent, renewing your mind in right thinking, sending demons to flight. Not enough time, invoking His Spirit. Not enough time spent, fighting the good fight!

—Scripture Reference—
Romans 7:13–25

HOSTAGE

Motivation tells me to move, but this feeling in my stomach is keeping me still. Motives pure and strong but weakness has joined along. Achievement gives a thrill, but the threat of failure provokes a pause. Fear is holding me hostage! Binding my hands and feet. Holding me down in a stifling struggle. Trying to break free, but fear has control of me. Hypnotized, paralyzed consumed in things over-analyzed.

—Scripture References—
1 John 4:18, Luke 12:4–7

BEGIN AGAIN

I missed my beginning, the original plan and view. Wish I never messed up the first time and wanted to start anew. Wish I got it right from the start, then I wouldn't have messed up the second time too. Born again, my plans began but once again I still didn't win. Familiar sin crept back in; I reap the same consequence of my beginning. How much more evil shall I reap 'til good has a go? Doing good now, so with God, all things are possible! With God, I'm always winning and there is no ending! Slate wiped clean; all things made new. I made it back to the beginning!

—Scripture References—
Matthew 12:43–45, Revelation 21:5

THE PRIZE

I try not to be selfish, but self is all I know. The truth is I can be ruthless if it comes down to me or you. Carnal cares scream out, "self-preservation!" common sense tells you to do whatever needs to be done to get the battle won. Two people starving with one piece of chicken, I know I'm going to be eating! All these things made perfect sense to me, until I found someone that, instead of selfishness, became a sacrifice so that I could have life. Showed me the power of love, and what it means to become a part of the grander theme. Living for giving, total sacrifice even if it means giving your life. I know this goes totally contrary to common sense. True understanding is only recognized when eyes are opened, surprised to realize, this life is not the prize!

—Scripture References—
James 3:13–16, Romans 12:1 and 2, 2 Timothy 1:7, Matthew 6:19–21

KILL IT

He kill 'em with their love, He kill 'em with their love! All day everyday flowers in bloom turn to dead buds. Worrying about life, love turns into fear. Responses to responsibility turns love into legality. Care for our loved ones turns to fear. Stewards over our children, responsibility is placed on me! Stewards over my entire family, does that all fall on me? Steward over the evil in me, control takes a toll when evil takes control of me. Am I the evil I see, can I be the worst in me? Faith in the Almighty in a fallen land turns to fear of our outcome. The sum of all truths, fear of God is the beginning of wisdom. Just like the fallen angels, we betray our creator day by day. Redemption came to mention on the sons of disobedience. Deliverance, forgiveness for the past born anew. Time to get back in line knowing the future has a chosen few. The past masses didn't pass the test. God's elect cannot respect or follow the world. Remnant restored, thanking the Lord for another chance. I dance and praise God now, though love has not yet been perfected in obedience toward the object of my affection. Glorifying God, the only direction! Perfect in me, purge the rest burned in the fiery furnace. Until we're made magnificent, glorified and innocent, His Grace will be sufficient. Never understood pain, with a thorn in my side something evil remains. A demon corrupting my mind and body. Salvation instantaneous but sanctification a process. Necessary to kill the wrong in me, so my path can be counted righteous at the last trumpet call. All said and done, the victory I've won made me in participation with creation's Glory. Now I see why it was meant to be so much pain and division, to bring me to the head, body anointed to reconnect with the Son. Kill it, everything that brings derision! Kill it and bring me back into Your bosom!

—Scripture References—
2 Timothy 1:7, Proverbs 1:7 and 29:25

VICTORY

The tower is raised up high, the mantle, it passes by. Bystanders begin to cry, victory! The band is jamming loud, every part is perfectly played. Elated is the crowd, in victory! Victory, Vic-tor-eee ahhh, there's nothing else I can see, say victory! More people are being drawn in, the stage has been set, the celebration can now begin, in victory! Remiss this story would be, if the honored guest was not at the party, thank Glory be Him we see, in victory! Victory, Vic-tor-eee ahhh, there's nothing else I can see, say victory! They pierced Him in His side, He hung, bled and He died, Jesus rose from the grave, now everybody can say, victory! Heavenly hosts have all joined in, this joy will never end. Hallelujah, Glory, Grace has finally placed me in victory!

—Scripture References—
Ephesians 1:20–23, 1 John 5:4, 1 Corinthians 15:57, Revelation 11:15–18

CONFLICT

I heard a voice inside my head. It said, "I just wish I were dead!" Doesn't make sense saying that to myself, but if I didn't say it, who did? I tossed and turned in my bed with conflict, turmoil and dread. Was I wrestling with myself, or some other entity I could not see? Alone, in the still quiet and it was screaming out at me! So quiet and calm, it was alarming. All alone, but something is talking to me. What could this entity be that I cannot see? I heard a voice in my head. It said, "I can't take any more! Problems break down the front door, break in the back door! Flooding the floor, rising until I'm drowning! I can't take it anymore!" I went to bed praising, raising my hands and thanking God for my many blessings. So how can I now be hearing these contrary contradictions to my aforementioned affirmations? I am convinced it is an evil entity on assignment, out to get me! I refute and cast down every thought of the enemy! God would not, will not put on me more than I'm able to carry! If The storms keep raging in my life and the waves rise high, He's given me the ability to swim and I'm anchored in Him! Though we walk through the valley of the shadow of death, let me tell you one thing. I cannot, will not fear any evil, because death has lost its sting! The King of kings has the keys to death and the grave. Since He saved my soul, He also holds the key to my heart. Evil entity, you must get back and behave! Calm and peace restored, feeling the joy of the Lord! Now, I sense an entity, identity, Holy, sent to me, to be my comfort and guide. Though He sits high upon the throne, I'm reminded that I'm never alone and one day we'll be truly united into one family!

—Scripture References—
2 Corinthians 12:1–10, Ephesians 1:3–5, Psalm 23:4, 1 Corinthians 15:55

DESTINY

Placed here to face fear and eradicate it! To shine the light of truth and love into dark places. Exposing lies devils implant behind our eyes. Reproving God's truth in the light. Turn fear on the enemy to give them a fright. I hear the blowing of the horn in the distance. Getting closer to my destiny, and it's feeling magnificent. But something's different. Giants on the ground, assigned to take me down. Slipping through, I always knew I was born for much more. Closer and closer, the greater the opposer. Now I'm here, knocking on heaven's door. Still I see, there is nothing but devils around, trying to keep me from my destiny. The monkey on my back is on the attack like a gorilla. The thorn in my side, like hooks digging in. Slashing, thrashing, bashing relentlessly! Trying to keep me from my destiny. The pressure, the pain, almost debilitating! Though my goal, never abating. Still I stand! Will not relent until all has been spent until I achieve my destiny!

—Scripture References—
John 3:21, Mark 13:13

TECH

"Is technology the devil?" As I pose this question, in reflection. At a time when people reveled over simple, rudimentary technologies, harnessing energy to make hard tasks easy, able to work more efficiently, there was a certain Amish community that shunned technology, calling it "the devil!" Certain Quakers took this same stance too, considering the invention of the TV quite abominable. Though these claims seemed absurd, at the time, and far left wing, recent technology has shaped our community into something that's taken us far from God. Family, not what it used to be. Technology may not be the devil, but the devil is definitely using technology. Not for mere education and entertainment but enslavement! Cameras on every corner, every cell phone. Satellites in space. Someone, somewhere has their eyes on you! Pseudo-omnipresence ringing true with the prince of the air everywhere! Forced to keep up with the Jones. Updated daily, leaving your technology outdated so quickly. Progress, inevitable, but moving so fast something's always lost along the way. On the other hand, the riches of a wicked man are stored up for the righteous. We have used and can use these means for the glory of God. An argument Christians have debated. Technology, got to love it, got to hate. Technology, what will be our fate with it?

—Scripture References—
Judges 2:19; Ecclesiastes 7:29; Psalm 81:12, 99:8, 106:29, 106:39; Revelation 13:16–18

WHY WORRY

"I wonder what tomorrow brings. Where will I be in a year? Ten years from now, how will I look? Will I work the same job, still married to Bob? My children, will they finish school, find a good life for themselves? Hope they never get caught up in dangerous vices. When they leave the house, how will I fill my time? I wonder when these gas prices will stop going up?" Daydreaming, worrying, with the future on my mind. Excessive worrying carries you away to a darker place. Forced to face more than God put on your plate. Stress kills, and the devil steals by replacing your love and faith with worry and doubt. Don't worry about anything, but pray about everything with thanksgiving. Thanking God in advance that your needs have been met. Your father may have abandoned you. Your husband may have cheated too. All types of bad things have happened, leaving you apprehensive about the future. Have to believe, all things have been, and still will be, working together for your good if you love the Lord. Your heavenly Father's track record, impeccable! He's brought you this far. Been right there with you, wherever you are. One day at a time, with Him, you will win! "So tell me again, why was I worrying?"

—Scripture References—
Matthew 6:25–34, Philippians 4:6 and 7

POWER OF HIS WORD (PART 1)

Looking up and out into the night, I begin to think. Stars shining bright, sky immense. So great, so vast, so in sync. Held together in place by forces we don't see. Things called gravity. Such a great God! Same God created you and I. With things so big out there in the sky, floating around in the atmosphere, why does He care about you and I? So tiny, so weak. Wrapped up in this sinful mess called flesh. Continuing with my thought process, I considered things much smaller than me. Much consideration brought me to the smallest entity of matter, an atom. The building blocks of all material life. How can it be, I'm made up of the same basic things as a tree or a bee? Unfathomably, you cannot be telling me that even inanimate objects share the same basic make up! Taking this closer look is making me see this material world much differently. So what appears to be a solid floor are actually innumerable atoms or molecules vibrating at a frequency to give the illusion of solidity. Things so small are really what hold everything in place, not gravity! Easy to see a Great God in the big, great things above. Now, easy to see Him, even greater still, revealed in the infinitesimally small. God made it all in love. After much contemplation, leaning on my own understanding, I had to return to His Word. I stand corrected in my conclusion. Just read, just heard. Things are not kept in place by gravity or innumerable atoms. They're all held together by the power of His Word!

—Scripture References—
Colossians 1:15–20, Hebrews 1:2 and 3, Psalm 8

TIME AND SPACE (PART 2)

So, what are these molecules that make up every material thing, working together in verse, controlling the universe? It's energy and mass, vibrating really fast. The properties of mass and acceleration make up the fields of space and time. Remove mass from the equation, and you've found something quite sublime. Energy in its purest form, without any form or mass, is no longer confined to space and time! Beams of light from the sun actually stretch across the fabric of time and space, all the way down to shine on your face. Formless forms further verify life outside of this physical world, outside of time. If you think about it, time had to be created. Concepts like before and after on a linear timeline is stretched thin the, more I stretch my mind. If you go back to the beginning of time, what happened before then, what happened before then? Reaching the end of a linear timeline, what happens after that? The future, unattainable. The past, never retain-able. The present, ever fleeting. By the time you say the word "now," it has already become "then." Easy to see a created world created for us, but can you see it for what it really is? It was made that all things seen were made by that which cannot be seen in physical creation. Physical limitations blind us from our spiritual sight. God being Spirit, requires that we worship Him in spirit and in truth. See through your eyes of faith, walk by faith, until that day you get to see Him face to face!

—Scripture References—
John 4:24, 8:12, 9:5, 12:46; Revelation 22:16; Malachi 4:1–3; Matthew 5:14

GOD'S OWN HEART

Coil and spring, pressed together, bend and go! Getting closer with every leap and bound. Effort is futile, though. Still fall back down to the cursed ground! Why am I so low? Can't reach Him in this sack of bones. Down here watching men live their lives without any care for the hereafter, but there is nothing here for me. They stay sinking in quicksand while I somehow stand, anchored on The Stone. Desire resonating in my soul. Need to reconnect with His Spirit. Need to be made whole. Then I can finally arrive at The Throne. Rising in spirit, falling in flesh. Look to the hills for some help, or at least a little taste. Instead, falling short with another test. Yearning and searching, yet isolated and alone. I wonder, will my time ever arrive? Knew it would take every bit of every part, with every pain a work of art. But He pursued me first. Written in each and every verse. Now God will be the first cause in my every desire. My love, my strength, my all in all! I will endure everything it takes to make it back to Him again! To make it to the end, you must go back to the start. Man of God, chasing after God's own heart.

—Scripture References—
Acts 4:11, Luke 6:38, Genesis 3:17, Romans 8:27, 1 Samuel 13:14, Acts 13:23, Jeremiah 1:5, Psalm 40:2, Matthew 7:24–27